# FRIEND of a FRIEND

**INTRODUCING YOUR
FRIENDS TO JESUS**

PETER SONDERGELD

Friend of a Friend: Introducing your friends to Jesus

Copyright © 2025 by Peter Sondergeld

Published by: Peter Sondergeld Ministries 11 Moffatt St, Toowoomba, Queensland, Australia

All rights reserved.

No part of this publication may be reproduced, stored in a retrieval system or transmitted in any form or by any means, electronic, mechanical, photocopying, recording or otherwise, without prior permission of Peter Sondergeld.

Unless otherwise indicated, Scripture quotations taken from The Holy Bible, New International Version® NIV®

Copyright © 1973, 1978, 1984, 2011 by Biblica, Inc.

Used with permission. All rights reserved worldwide.

ISBN 978-0-6454034-1-1

To Angela and Jesus – thanks for
being my friend and for teaching me
how to be one

"I read Friend of a Friend twice. The first time, I wanted to know my friend Jesus better. I also wanted to know my friends better and gather a few more of them. Then someone mentioned that the book made him smile. So I read it again and smiled my way through it. Talking about friends will do that."

> **Ed Welch**, Psychologist and faculty member of the Christian Counselling Foundation, author of numerous books including *When People Are Big and God Is Small*, *Shame Interrupted*, *Side by Side*, and *Created to Draw Near*.

"There are few things more important in our present cultural moment of us-versus-them tribalism, than learning from Jesus what it means to be known as a "friend of sinners" (Luke 7:34). In Friend of a Friend, Peter Sondergeld helps us to uncomplicate evangelism by teaching us how to be better friends ourselves — firstly as those who experience a richer friendship with Jesus, and then secondly as those who extend genuine friendship to those around us. In each of these chapters is biblical and practical wisdom for every follower of Jesus!"

> **Adam Ramsey**, Lead Pastor at Liberti Church, Gold Coast, Australia; Director for Acts 29 Asia Pacific; author of a few books, including *Honour*, *Faithfully Present*, and *Truth on Fire: Gazing at God until Your Heart Sings*.

Peter sits with us, like a fellow traveller and the best of guides. He's made mistakes but learned from them. He's walked the paths on which he's leading us. By bringing the scriptures to light and sharing stories from personal experience, Peter helps us see our neighbours and ourselves as Jesus sees us. Our hearts enliven, our practices mature, and our love grows.

> **Zack Eswine**, co-founder of Sage Christianity, and author of *Wiser with Jesus* and *The Imperfect Pastor*.

In this enjoyable, easy to read, book on evangelism, Peter uses the metaphor of "friendship" to turn evangelism, as we usually think of it, on its head! As I read each chapter, I found myself responding very differently to a lot of the other books I have read on evangelism. I found myself saying, "Now that is easy. I think I could do that kind of evangelism." If you want to grow in this area of your life or you want to unleash a church to be more at ease with sharing their faith in Jesus, I would highly recommend this book.

> **Dr. Tim S. Lane**, President: Institute for Pastoral Care, author of *How People Change* and *Unstuck: A Nine Step Journey to Change That Lasts*.

"Friend of a Friend is warm, conversational, and deeply challenging. With pastoral sensitivity, theological depth, and everyday wisdom, this book invites readers to meet Jesus and discover the richness of authentic friendship. Thank you, Peter, for this helpful work that points us to our truest friend, and how that motivates all other friendships."

**Malcolm Gill** (PhD, Dallas Theological Seminary), Lead Pastor, Multicultural Bible Ministry Sydney, author of *Knowing Who You Are* and *Topical Preaching in a Complex World*.

"Peter has a rare gift for seeing what's really going on beneath the surface. In Friend of a Friend, he helps us see that our struggle with evangelism often comes down to this—we don't really know how to be good friends. By pointing us to Jesus, the ultimate friend of sinners, Peter invites us to rediscover the joy of friendship that naturally leads to sharing our faith. If you are tired of evangelistic approaches that are impersonal and leave you feeling guilty, then I highly recommend you read Friend of a Friend."

**Timon Bengtson**, (ThM Dallas Theological Seminary), State Co-ordinator for Christian Community Churches Qld, Lead Pastor, Brookside Community Church

"My fuel tank for both friendship and evangelism often feels like it is running on empty. Yet, in this book—full of Peter's pastoral warmth and biblical wisdom, and beautifully pointing towards the friendship of Jesus—I've received a high octane refuelling. Meaningful friendships that share Christ feel more attainable and more exciting than ever. Get ready for a top-up!"

**Ste Casey**, Pastor Speke Baptist church, Liverpool, UK, Tutor and Speaker for Biblical Counselling UK, author of *I Prayed and Nothing Changed*.

# CONTENTS

| | | |
|---|---|---|
| Introduction | | 9 |
| 1 | Our Problem with Friendship and Evangelism | 17 |
| 2 | Jesus is Our Solution | 17 |
| 3 | Jesus Enjoys Sinners | 39 |
| 4 | Jesus Walks with Sinners | 51 |
| 5 | Jesus Welcomes Interruptions by Sinners | 63 |
| 6 | Jesus is Personal with Sinners | 75 |
| 7 | Jesus Knows Sinners | 87 |
| 8 | Jesus Sees Sinners | 99 |
| 9 | Jesus Cares for Sinners | 111 |
| 10 | Jesus is Loyal to Sinners | 1213 |
| 11 | A Final Word | 135 |
| Endnotes | | 139 |

# My Story

## INTRODUCTION

I have to confess something.

I have had an awkward relationship with evangelism for most of my life.

Some of my wrestle with evangelism was personal. I was immature, the way I saw the world was skewed, and I was overly sensitive to other people's opinions. Evangelism always felt like conflict was at the centre of what I was called to accomplish – I had to show someone they were wrong. That's a tough ask for someone particularly concerned with what other people thought of them. But these personal dynamics of mine only accounted for a small portion of my problem. The larger portion of my troubles had to do with the church - the way the church viewed evangelism and the methods they used to engage in it.

I'm not saying I don't like evangelism, or that I don't think it is important. Jesus' command to share the good news is clear (Matthew 28:19-20), and the work which was done by him on the cross is the best news ever. It isn't called the gospel for nothing. But let's be honest, evangelism in the church can get a little weird sometimes. And it's not so much a problem with evangelism itself, it's what the church does (or has done) with it.

I want to start by telling you the story of my awkward relationship with evangelism with the expectation that some of you will be able to identify with some of the struggles I have had. As you read my story, I want you to know that my intention is not to vilify my upbringing, anyone I have interacted with, or any evangelistic methodology. My intention is to help you see how evangelism, a sacred honour of Christians, something we will never do again after Jesus returns, can become impersonal and get out of sync with who God is and who we truly are. God is personal and relational, we have been made in his image, and the best evangelism is personally and relationally rich.

## THE EARLY YEARS

I was born into the church. From my first breath up to this very day, my father has been a pastor. One of my key memories from my upbringing was its strong religious flavour. Religion has a tendency to divide people between good and bad, and our family was no different. We were the people on the right side of the line, on God's side, and we had to be good. Everyone who wasn't on our side was bad. We viewed everyone outside the church as inferior and operated on the basis that they needed to come and join us and do life our way. There was a strong 'us and them' feel to it. And we didn't have much to do with them other than telling them they should become like us.

This 'us and them' mentality fed directly into my understanding of how to do evangelism. Anyone around us who wasn't a Christian was always evil in some way. Even when they did something relatively good, we quickly cut it down with the assertion that their motives were dark and had irreparably stained whatever relatively good thing they may have done. Our task was to help them see how bad they were and how they could get out of trouble through the work of Jesus. While we had pity on them for the predicament they were in with God, we loved them from a distance. We weren't side by side with them, and we weren't close friends with them. Far from it, we needed to be careful of them and the influence they could wield over us. It wasn't very personal, and it wasn't particularly loving or gracious.

## LATE TEENS

As I grew up, my perception of evangelism became more nuanced. I sat under preaching which taught me that we were to be in but not of the world. What this meant for us was that we were to be moving in a centrifugal direction, away from the institution of the church and towards the lost with the news of the gospel. The siege mentality of my younger years would not do. Jesus wanted us to be salt and light. We had to get amongst it. And we did. We door knocked, we gave away bibles, and we looked for opportunities to share the gospel with people.

We were regularly encouraged to be missional. Many of the churches I attended ran training courses on how to do evangelism well. And while most of the training courses were helpful, I couldn't seem to shake the nagging thought that the best evangelists I ever saw were those who were untrained – new Christians.

Lots of good gospel activity happened in this time. Many people heard about Jesus and some people became Christians. But in the midst of all of this, something happened which unsettled me. The pastor of the church I was attending wrote a 6-week evangelism training course which he led the church through. In the course we had to choose someone who would be our evangelism project for the duration of the study. We committed to actively pray for them and seek an opportunity to share the gospel with them. I could see that my pastor meant well, but it seemed weird to me, and very impersonal. The person we were trying to reach became a task or an objective to us, and we manoeuvred in the relationship in the hope we would get to a point where we would have the opportunity to share the gospel with them. Instead of the ebb and flow of a genuine relationship, it felt unnatural and forced, and if I am honest, a little relationally manipulative.

My approach to evangelism had matured a little, but it still lacked the nuance and breadth it needed. My whole strategy revolved around moving non-Christians relationally to the place where I could share the gospel with them. I was like a golfer who only had one club in their golf bag. No matter the situation, the goal was to

## Introduction

tell them the gospel message - they were sinners and they needed Christ's work on their behalf. I felt the pressure to move them to the point where I could talk about the gospel every time I spoke with them – the hard moments, the good ones, and everything in between.

I did get to share the gospel with some people, but many of them didn't respond positively and it left me not knowing what to do next. The gold standard was to share the gospel and have the person give their life to Jesus on the spot. But it didn't happen very often. I wondered what I had done wrong. I am a little embarrassed to admit it, but there were even times where I felt I couldn't be friends with them if they didn't accept Jesus. That thought horrifies me now.

### EARLY ADULTHOOD

As my life moved on, I became connected with churches who had an attractional approach to evangelism. These churches always put on a good show. They had lots of stage lighting, black walls and ceilings, loud bands, entertaining preachers, and regular altar calls. They were good at attracting non-Christians to church services and often talked about how many people had made decisions for Jesus.

At one service I attended they asked me if I would provide some pastoral counselling to those who had responded to an altar call to give their lives to Jesus. I enthusiastically said yes. The end of the sermon arrived. It had been funny, energetic, and many young adults came forward in response to the appeals of the preacher. I sat with one young man in his early 20s. He had responded to the invitation of the preacher. But as we talked together, I gradually realised he had no idea what he was responding to. It became clear to me that he had been hooked by the emotion and not by anything concrete. As far as I could tell, there wasn't anything personal going on between him and God. He had no clarity about who Jesus was, what sin was, or how he was supposed to respond. I had a lot of work to do. This attractional model of evangelism left me wanting something better.

## IN RECENT TIMES

About 10 years ago, my awkward relationship with evangelism began to change. I enrolled in some study which helped me to understand myself and other people in the light of scripture. My world turned from black and white into colour. As I studied the Bible, I saw with much greater clarity how God had designed humanity to operate. I saw how humanity was originally made to be relationally connected to God, how we operate properly when we stay in relationship with him, and how we go haywire without him. Before long, I began to see how I was made to connect to Jesus in every moment and every situation. It was a time of unparalleled spiritual growth.

This increased clarity about how to do relationship with Jesus and how he does relationship with me spilled over into my other relationships. What I was learning was far more significant than I realised. As I look back on it now, the problem I had for most of my life wasn't mainly an evangelism problem, it was mainly a friendship problem. I knew how to do tasks, I knew the standard God was calling us to, and I knew I was meant to be obedient. But I didn't know how to be a friend. The first time I saw it like this made me feel like I had failed grade one in school. It seemed like such a basic error. But Jesus, my teacher and friend, was helping me to learn what I felt like I should have known all along.

My conversations with non-Christians changed; they became *genuine* conversations between friends. I thought less about the message I was trying to get across and more about the other person and what they were saying. The assurance scripture had given me about the way God had designed humanity to be connected to Jesus meant I could relax and be present in every conversation. I figured that if I was good friends with Jesus and with the other person, then connecting them together at some point was inevitable. I was able to walk with my friend wherever the conversation went because we were all made for Jesus. When it comes to humanity, all roads lead to Rome – or in this case, Jesus. I didn't need to drag them to the gospel anymore, I just needed to be a good listener, and a good friend.

## FRIEND OF A FRIEND

This is the essence of friend of a friend evangelism. A friend of a friend is someone you don't know very well. It is someone your friend is close to whom you have connection with through them. Sometimes a friend of a friend becomes a friend directly, sometimes they don't. One of the strongest indicators of the likelihood of them becoming a friend of yours, is the closeness your mutual friend has to both you and them. The closer they are to both of you, the greater the likelihood that they will talk about and connect both of you together.

To the unsaved world, we are the friend and Jesus is the friend of a friend. As we deepen our friendship with Jesus and with those who don't know him, deeply personal and relationally rich ways to connect your friends to Jesus will naturally appear. This is the dynamic which makes friend of a friend evangelism go. It's that simple.

This is a book about the greatest friend I have ever had, the one who taught me how to be a friend. As you do friendship with him, you will learn how to make friends and be friends with non-Christians so you can introduce them to the One, True friend, Jesus.

# 1

# Our Problem with Friendship and Evangelism

Not long ago I was doing some teaching on Friend of a Friend at a local church. At the end of the first workshop, an older woman approached me and told me about some non-Christian people she had been friends with for over 20 years. She went on to reveal to me that despite their being friends for such a long time, she had never talked about Jesus with them. It was quite an admission. But it wasn't the first time I had heard one like that. In my time in the church I have heard more of these kinds of stories than I can count. I used to be one of them.

I wonder if you'd stop and think about her admission for a moment. I want to ask you this question:

*Is it an evangelism failure or is it a friendship failure?*

Some of you may be thinking I am being a little harsh by calling it a failure. But this was the nature of the conversation I was having with the woman. She was telling me something which she felt badly about. Something she should have done differently. But what was wrong? Was it an evangelism or a friendship failure?

Most of us probably think it was an evangelism failure. I used to. She should have shared the good news about Jesus with her friends before then. It's one of the reasons why you need to talk about Jesus early on in a friendship before it gets too hard. Some will think she needs more evangelism training - she needs to learn how to manoeuvre in conversations more effectively. Still others will think she needs to repent of her sin of not sharing the gospel with her friends. These may all be valid thoughts in and of themselves, but they miss the mark because they are all built upon the assumption it is an evangelism failure. But it isn't an evangelism failure.

*It's a friendship failure.*

Why? Because friendship is about walking together through life. It is about doing life together. It is about knowing and being known by one another. She was friends with these people and had walked with them for over 20 years, and she had never told them about what (or who) was most important to her. She hadn't let them in to that part of her life. I don't mean to be critical of her because I have done a similar thing in the past, but the reality is, she needed to be thinking more about the nature of her friendship than the failure in her evangelism.

## PROBLEMS AND SOLUTIONS

If you get the problem wrong, then you inevitably get the solution wrong. One follows the other. It's as true when you go to the doctor as it is when it comes to reaching a lost world with the gospel. It is my contention that the church has often misconstrued this woman's problem as an evangelism failure, and this misdiagnosis has led us up the garden path to solutions which don't deal with our core problem. We have written evangelism books, undertaken more evangelism training, and developed numerous evangelistic programs, which are good in themselves, but we haven't dealt with the core problem – the friendship problem. What we should have been doing is teaching people how to be good friends to those who don't know Jesus. If we had done this, then I suspect many more people would have heard about him.

Mischaracterising the problem as an evangelism problem rather than a friendship problem, changes the way we relate to others – they inevitably become a stepping stone to the achievement of another task. And tasks have a very strong gravitational pull. Now I am not saying there isn't a task in the mix here – there is. But our main problem here has to do with people, not a task. And when one focuses on achieving a task in the midst of what is essentially a people problem, we end up depersonalising others as they become a means to an end – the end of evangelism.

This subtle shift, a shift from person to task, changes the way we engage with others, and most non-Christians can pick it a mile away. They seem to be able to tell when we are selling something. This shouldn't be a surprise to us. This knack of being able to discern when someone is interested in us or mainly interested in something else, is not unique to evangelistic conversations, it is built into all of humanity. It is programmed into our personhood, a warning light if you like, that something other than a personal relationship is happening.

You have probably been in conversations yourself where you have noticed this dynamic in play. The conversation begins, and everything seems normal and genuine. But then a seed of doubt begins to grow in your mind. You start thinking, "What are they up to? There is something a little weird going on here. It doesn't feel normal." And it isn't. Somewhere, somehow, things shifted, and it wasn't about you and them anymore, it was about them and something else. All of a sudden you realised they had a hidden agenda, and you had become the means to another end. What you thought you were engaging in and what you *were* engaging in were two different things. Somewhere along the line, the personal nature of what you were engaged in had drained out. I have heard so many stories about these kinds of evangelistic interactions.

## IT'S PERSONAL

This task-oriented approach to evangelism is in stark contrast to the very nature of what we are doing in partnering with God to reach a fallen world. When you bring a fresh pair of eyes and look closely at what Jesus has sent us to do, you can see how it is richly personal from beginning to end.

The centrepiece of God's mission to rescue a fallen

world involved the second person of the Trinity coming close. He had come close on occasion when God visibly showed up in the Old Testament, but this time it was different, completely different. This time, he took on human flesh and became an embryo, then a baby, then a child, a teenager, and at last an adult. It was so close and so personal, that no one expected it.

He ended up physically walking on earth for 33 years. He grew up with people, worked with them, talked with them, and helped them. His life culminated in the offering of himself as an atonement for humanity's sin on the cross. He paid our debt so we could be forgiven. If you are a Christian, then you are likely well versed in this truth. But don't miss the personal direction to it, because the gospel is not merely about the payment of a debt - as precious as that is. The ultimate purpose of the gospel is about humanity being reconciled to God. (1 Peter 3:18) Jesus didn't die only to forgive our sins, he died to restore us back to relationship with God, he died in order that God's estranged children could be adopted back into the family, he died to bring the outcasts back in. It is so personal.

Then he sent us - *us* - to communicate this message. (Matthew 28:18-20) That in itself is amazing. There have been more than a few people throughout history who have wondered about this strategy. I mean, stop for a moment and think about all of the different ways God could have communicated this message to the world. He could have used social media or TV or even invented another medium before its time to distribute the message.

But he didn't. His plan was and is people, humanity, personal beings telling the good news. It's stunning.

Then there is the message we have been sent to communicate to the world – they need to repent and believe in Jesus. This kind of language is so familiar to most people in the church that we can forget how radically personal it is. The essence of what we are calling people to do is recognise how their sin is a personal offence to God, say sorry to him, ask for his forgiveness, place their trust in him, and walk with him for the rest of their lives. This is what repenting and believing is. Can you see how personal it is? It's no wonder the difficult task of recognising you are wrong and saying sorry has become comedic fodder for countless shows and movies. It is a very personal thing to do.

Once someone has repented and believed in Jesus, the third person of the Trinity, the Holy Spirit, takes up residence in them. They become his home. And one of the many good things he gets up to in the lives of those who have turned to Jesus, is the way he works in us to cause us to cry out Abba Father. (Romans 8:15-16) It turns out that God is not happy with us merely being his children, he wants us to have the experience of being his children at the depths of our being – such a personal dynamic.

Here's where we are: the second person of the Trinity came close by taking on human flesh, he dwelt with us (John 1:14) for 33 years, died on a cross to reconcile and restore our relationship with God, sent us to reach a fallen world, taught us to call the world to repent and believe in him, with the objective of the third person of the Trinity living in us and causing us to cry out Abba Father. Can you see it? God's mission is personal from beginning to end.

I could go on. There is much more to say. But suffice to say at this point that if God's mission is personal in nature, then we would do well to engage in it using the most personal of methods. And there is nothing more personal than friendship – friendship with Jesus and friendship with those who don't know him yet.

Friend of a friend isn't a new strategy or technique to help you achieve the task of evangelism. It is about deepening your relationships and making you a better friend. As you do, you will find it won't just be your relationships with non-Christians which will change, your relationships with everyone will change because you will become a better friend to everyone around you. Along the way you will become much more adept at connecting Jesus in natural ways to all of your friends.

## YOU SHOULD MEET MY FRIEND

One of my best mates is a guy called Kurt. I first met him in 2013. In 2014 we decided we would travel together to Philadelphia to undertake some onsite study. It turned out to be a really significant trip which connected us as friends.

Kurt and I don't hold anything back from each other. From the darkest grittiest things right through to the big celebrations. Nothing is off limits. We are fiercely loyal to one another and don't hesitate to speak the truth in loving and constructive ways. I love and value him deeply. He has been and continues to be a rich encouragement to me. Whenever I write something he is usually the first one to read it. I know he will be honest with me and tell me what he thinks - always for my good. I wouldn't be able to count the number of times God has powerfully used his words in my life.

I talk about Kurt a lot to my other friends. A couple of months ago he preached at my church. Some people joked about how good it was to meet my imaginary friend. They had heard me talk about this 'Kurt' but had never seen him. I was glad they got to meet him and glad he was able to minister to the people in the church I lead.

Sometimes, when I am listening to people talk about their life and the troubles they are facing, I begin to think of Kurt. "Oh, I wish you could meet Kurt. You would really like him. You and he would have a great conversation about this stuff. He would be more helpful to you than I am. You should talk to him." Sometimes I have even said these things to people. But it doesn't help much because Kurt lives in Sydney and is rarely in my hometown. It is more of a wish than anything.

This is the kind of conversation I am suggesting you could be having with your non-Christian friends. It will start in a similar place, a close present tense friendship with Jesus, but will end in a much better place because Jesus is not stuck in Sydney. He is in you and is not far from your non-Christian friends. (Acts 17:27)

So lean in and take the opportunities when they come.

### Our Problem with Friendship and Evangelism

And when you get the chance, tell your friend, "Oh, I so want you to meet my friend Jesus. He is so good. You would really like him."

> The first thing Andrew did was to find his brother Simon and tell him, "We have found the Messiah" (that is, the Christ). And he brought him to Jesus.
>
> John 1:41–42

### FOR REFLECTION AND DISCUSSION

1) How have you engaged in evangelism in the past? What approaches have you used?

2) How personal is your relationship with Jesus? Would you use the category 'friendship' to describe the way you relate to each other?

3) Can you think of a time where you treated people less personally because you were focused on achieving a task? How does the gospel keep us warmly personal?

# 2

# Jesus is Our Solution

Maxims abound in our culture.

*Follow your heart.*

*A change is as good as a holiday.*

*Better a bird in the hand than two in the bush.*

They are pithy little sayings which capture a general truth or principle without saying everything there is to say about the topic. Here is a well-known maxim about friendship:

*You have to be a friend to have a friend.*

Have you ever heard this one? Has anyone ever said it to you?

I have heard it. It was said to me more times than I can count. Those who said it to me intended for it to spur me on, but it never did, because they only ever lobbed it at me when I was struggling to find and form good friendships. Their intention was to assist me, but it never helped. It only ever sounded like a criticism to me. I never thanked them for saying it, I was too distracted by the need to suppress my frustration to do that.

## FRIENDSHIP IS SELF-EVIDENT

Despite the problematic nature of the way this maxim is sometimes used, it does assume something which is generally true about humanity – almost everyone knows what a friend is. It doesn't really matter where you learnt it or how you know it, for most people, friendship is self-evident. We all have some idea of what it is and the way it is supposed to operate. Narcissists, haters, and toxic people can abound, friends can betray us, and we can be left alone, yet even then, most of us still have some idea about how friendships are meant to work - or at the very least, how they are not meant to work.

The self-evident nature of friendship can be seen in culture too. We watch story after story about friendship in movies, stage productions, and television shows which have been written to resonate with our deep intuitions about the nature and value of it. And by and large, they get it pretty right. One of them was even called Friends. No one needs to tell us what a healthy friendship is, we seem to know it when we see it, and our reactions are the evidence of it.

Scripture seems to assume we have a reasonable handle of what it is too. Given the centrality of friendship to living life the way God intended, one would expect to find long sections of scripture which teach us explicitly about how to be a good friend. But we don't. While there are lots of passages about how to do relationships in general, there are relatively few about how to do friendship. It does pop up from time to time and there are a few passages which deal with it in some detail (such as John 15), but by and large, scripture seems to assume you know the basics about what it is and how it works.

## FRIENDSHIP PROBLEMS

Despite the self-evident nature of friendship and the presence of all these things which run so heavily in our favour, our ability to form and do friendships is pretty ordinary. You don't need to have too many conversations with others to learn that friendships don't come along as frequently as many of us would like, they break down very easily, and loneliness is more widespread than most of us want to admit. A recent announcement by the World Health Organisation said that loneliness is a "priority public health problem and policy issue across all age groups" because of its effect on "physical and mental health, quality of life, and longevity."[1] If you have a few hours to spare and enjoy opening cans of worms, then ask those around you about what they think true friendship is, how many true friends they have, and what friendship problems they have encountered. Sadly, I think the answers would be discouraging.

Interestingly, the church hasn't done much better. While there are some who have found deeper and richer friendships in the church than they ever had outside of it, there are many within it who have struggled to form healthy, deep friendships – myself included. I have heard people in the church say that they love one another even though they don't really like each other, and it has left me wondering what that even means. I have seen them fail to follow through on some of the most basic friendship practices (such as following up after someone has shared something difficult which was going on in their life). I have noticed many people in the church having better friendships with those outside of it than those inside of it. The church isn't immune to friendship struggles. Far from it.

The obvious question at this point is: What is the problem? If friendship is mostly self-evident, why do we struggle so much with it? In order to answer this, you need to go back to humanity's original design. Take a close look at Genesis and you will see how relationality is central to who we are as image bearers – we were made to be in relationship with God and others. (Genesis 1:27,5:3) Our relationship with God is meant to inform and shape every other one. (Matthew 22:37)

But as the story goes, humanity turned away from God in the Garden, and when we did, our relationality became disordered. (Genesis 3) We ended up living a life of contradictions. We know what we are supposed to be doing but we can't always do it. Being relational by design leaves us knowing what friendship looks like and how to do it, but the disordering which has happened leaves us unable to consistently live it out.

One of the key reasons why it is so hard for us to live

it out comes down to the DNA of indwelling sin. Sin, by its very nature, is antisocial. It is opposed to friendship. You only have to look at the consequences of the fall of humanity to see that. Those who were once seamlessly connected to God and each other – Adam and Eve – curved in on themselves and ended up at odds with one another and with God. (Genesis 3:8-13) We shouldn't be too surprised. It's not rocket science. You can't be a selfish person and have lots of friends. It just doesn't work that way.

## FRIENDSHIP HELP

We can address some of our struggle with friendship by learning the guidelines and principles of friendship. Just a few keystrokes and the click of a button and we will have more information than we can read in a lifetime. But despite its helpfulness, it doesn't ultimately get us where we want to go, because it doesn't deal with our inability to consistently *apply* what we already know. Learning how to do friendship by learning the theory of it is like learning how to swim by watching YouTube videos. Guidelines and principles will only get you so far. At some point you have to get in. At some point you need to dive into it and engage with it in practice.

What we really need is a friend, a great friend, an amazing friend. We need a friend who will do friendship with us in a way that will teach us how to be a friend to others. Someone who won't be repelled or put off by our selfish tendencies and will continue to walk with us at our worst. Someone who by their friendship with us will settle the fluctuations in the way we do friendship. Someone who has experienced the brokenness of friendship in a fallen world and knows how to navigate through it. Someone who can be a friend even when they are getting nothing out of it.

Who would that be? Well, you probably know the answer. It's Jesus. He is a great friend to you. He is the best friend you have ever had or will ever have. You may not know it, you may not see it, or it may be a new thought for you, but it is true nonetheless – Jesus is the best friend.

As we look at the way he does friendship in the remainder of this book, there will be times when you will read about him doing exactly what you would expect and other times when he will surprise you. In large part this is a function of the diverse person he is - king, judge, Lord, Messiah *and* friend. Seeing these together in the same person can be challenging to get your head around, especially when you realise that this mighty friend has chosen to be friends with sinners. You will never find a more head-spinning or amazing description of the kind of friend Jesus is than this: Jesus, a friend of sinners.

## A FRIEND OF SINNERS

*Friend of sinners.*

Never before has such a cutting insult meant so much to so many.

*Friend of sinners.*

It was a label Jesus' opponents gave him – probably behind his back. But it wasn't the only thing they said. Here's the rest of it.

> 'Look at him! A glutton and a drunkard, a friend of tax collectors and sinners!'
>
> Luke 7:34

It was a well-timed insult which they thought described the kind of person Jesus was. It was something which was meant to sideline him - a slur on his good reputation. That he was a slave to his stomach, a drunken fool, someone who spent too much time with sinners. The critics were the ones who were self-assured. They had their religion sorted out. They knew the laws, they kept away from bad people, and they had no use for the friendship Jesus offered. They didn't need him.

But for those who knew they were a mess, for those who knew they didn't have their lives together, for every person throughout history whose troubles and brokenness have loomed large in their face, for everyone who hasn't fit in or made the grade, there have never been more sublime words:

*Jesus, the friend of sinners.*

Slow down. Soak in the thought. Do you count yourself a sinner? Can you see the mess you have caused in your life? Then you need to know you have a friend. And he is a good friend. He is a great friend. He is the perfect friend.

## OUTSIDER TO INSIDER

Friend of sinners - countless authors have been inspired by this nickname given to Jesus. In the centuries that have followed, much has been written about how Jesus' death on the cross for sinners is the greatest act of friendship ever. And it is. But this is not what Jesus' opponents meant when they levelled this insult at him. What they were referring to was his association with those who didn't fit in, those who weren't up to scratch, those who were non-compliant, those who were in a different category to the one they were in. But they misunderstood something critical. These people were Jesus' specialty.

Sin puts you on the outer. It always does. This mechanism began in the Garden of Eden and has echoed throughout human history. Take a wrong step, make a bad choice, give into temptation, and you end up on the outer. Everyone does. The great irony about Jesus' critics is that they were on the outer as much as any of the sinners were, yet they couldn't see it. It was this very dynamic which made their condition so much more dangerous than those they were distancing themselves from.

But Jesus was different. As the only perfect man, he was the only true insider. Everyone else was an outsider – religious people included. Sin had made them this way. They didn't measure up to God's standards as revealed in scripture and were on the wrong side of the law. But far from distancing himself from them, this was the very reason he had come. Look across the gospels and you will see Jesus being a friend to many. (Matthew 26:50, Luke 5:20, John 11:11) He was a friend to outsiders in order to bring them back to God.

If you are a Christian today, it is because Jesus was a friend to you when you were an outsider. He came alongside you at your worst and he gave you the opportunity to enter into friendship with him. And the good news is that his outsider to insider friendship approach didn't end when you became a Christian. If it did, then we would all be in trouble. He is well aware we will have indwelling sin until we die, or he returns. He knows we will need him to be the friend of sinners a few more times yet.

There is no better way to learn how to be a friend of sinners than to have Jesus as your friend. As we experience his detailed and faithful friendship of us at a personal level, we will become clearer about how we can be a friend, and more consistent in how we do friendship with those around us. You can't enter into close friendships with everyone, but if you keep your eyes on Jesus, you will learn how to be a friend to anyone.

When Jesus began his ministry, no one believed him, no one was his friend. But by the time he had finished, he had a small number of friends which continues to grow to this very day. Since then, many other people have discovered they have a friend in Jesus and have decided to be his friend too. For most of them, they found out who

Jesus was through a friend. It may have been a long-term friend, or a short-term friend, or even someone who was a friend to them for a particular moment in time. It doesn't really matter how deep the friendship was; for most people, Jesus started out as a friend of a friend.

My intention in the first part of this book was to clear away some of the debris in the church regarding evangelism and friendship. I did this so you would be able to clearly see how Jesus is a friend of sinners. In the remainder of the book we will look at all of the wonderful ways Jesus does friendship with outsiders, and how his friendship of them informs and shapes the way we can be a friend to them too. As we deepen our friendships with Jesus and with those who don't know him, we will inevitably connect the two of them together and they will hopefully want to become friends with him also.

> While Jesus was having dinner at Matthew's house, many tax collectors and sinners came and ate with him and his disciples.
>
> Matthew 9:10

## FOR REFLECTION AND DISCUSSION

1) How would you describe what a true friend is? How many true friends do you have?

2) What is your experience of friendship in the church?

3) Where did you/can you learn how to be a friend?

# 3

# Jesus Enjoys Sinners

I was once a high school teacher.

For those who don't know, there are two pivotal events in a high school teacher's life which determine much of their happiness for the upcoming school year: the allocation of the classes they will teach and where they fall on the timetable. If you are allocated good classes and they are scheduled at times which are conducive to learning, then you are normally set up for a good year. If you aren't, then you could well be in for a tough one.

One of the time slots almost every high school teacher dreads are the lessons after lunch on a Friday. I used to call them the graveyard shift. Most teachers want to avoid these if they can. I was no different.

So, here I was at the beginning of what turned out to be my second last year of teaching, waiting with bated breath for the timetable to be handed out. I received my copy and immediately noticed I had been allocated two year 7 Christian Studies classes, one after the other, on Friday after lunch. And in case you don't know, it is quite a challenge to teach students in a Christian school about Jesus because of their exposure to it at home, church, youth, and almost every other class at school. As the saying goes, it is a little like carrying coal to Newcastle (a major coal producing English city). My heart sank. They were big classes with over 30 students in each. It was going to be an uphill climb. But I had no choice, so I resolved to make the most of it.

The Friday of the first week of school rolled around and before I knew it the end-of-lunch bell had sounded. It was time for the first lesson. I walked into the classroom slightly on edge and a little more vigilant than normal. But as the lesson played out, something surprising happened. I began to enjoy the students in the class. I feared they would be difficult and painful, but instead, they were enjoyable.

Before the lesson finished, I told them how much I was enjoying them. Their spirits lifted even more, and they became even easier to teach. In that moment, a penny dropped; something clicked for me in a way it never had before. My enjoyment of them was feeding into the way they related to me. It seemed that the more I enjoyed them, the easier they were to teach. I began to see a similar yet opposite dynamic at work in teachers who clearly disliked their classes. Their attitude toward their classes influenced how the students interacted with them, but in ways which were not helpful at all. They had no end of trouble.

While this class wasn't perfect, far from it, I resolved to tell them I liked being with them each week. It became part of my greeting at the beginning of each lesson I had with them. "Boy, I like teaching this class. I really enjoy being with you all." They liked being liked. Who doesn't? It ended up being one of the most enjoyable classes I have ever taught in my teaching career. The more I liked being with them, the more they seemed to like me too. My enjoyment of them was the bedrock beneath every lesson I had with them that year. I had learnt something about people in that class which had application far beyond the educational context. It was something which would make its way into every relationship I had.

Liking and enjoying people is an essential part of every friendship. If you can't find something to enjoy about others then you won't even get started when it comes to friendship. But if you like the other person and enjoy being with them, then a key part of the foundation of a friendship has been laid. It is one of the main dynamics which makes them go.

It may cause a car accident in your head, but when I read the gospels, I can't help but think that Jesus enjoyed being with sinners. Perhaps even, that Jesus enjoyed sinners. Now, I am not saying he enjoyed the sin they had committed or were engaged in, but it seems to me that he enjoyed being with those who were on the outer, those who didn't measure up, those who couldn't pull their lives together. They seemed to be his kind of people. Clearly, it was something which came as quite a surprise to many.

## JESUS ENJOYED SINNERS

While Jesus was morally perfect, his reputation amongst the religious people of the day was far from it. One only needs to remember the derogatory nickname 'friend of sinners' to know that. (Luke 7:34) As far as they were concerned, Jesus was a bad person who hung out with bad people.

At the core, a bad reputation is really just another way of talking about shame. When it comes to bad reputations or shame, the focus isn't so much on what you have done but on who you are – your identity. You have a connection to sin or evil in one way or another and it says something about you - you are dirty, unclean, and worthless.

But if Jesus was sinless, if he was perfect, then how did *he* end up with a bad reputation? How did he end up being affected by shame? The answer to this can be found by understanding how shame works. At a foundational level, shame is connected to sin. Whenever you or I sin, shame comes along with it. But shame is highly contagious too. You don't have to be a sinner to experience shame, you only need to be personally connected to those who have it to catch it. It rubs off onto anyone who associates with shame-filled people.

Jesus was spending so much time with the 'big sinners' that their shame was rubbing off on him. He hadn't done anything wrong, but the amount of time he spent with them said something about who he was – as far as the religious leaders were concerned anyway. I suspect that if we were him, many of us within the church would have

## Jesus Enjoys Sinners

probably spent just enough time with the big sinners to show them how they were wrong and how to get back to a good place. But not Jesus. He sat down with them and ate and drank – a personal sign of his acceptance of them – without compromising his integrity.

One of the most beautiful expressions of this happens immediately after the calling of Matthew the tax collector. (Matthew 9:9-13) Jesus walked past Matthew when he was sitting at his tax collector booth and called him to follow him. His call was so powerful that Matthew immediately got up and followed him.

Not long afterwards, Matthew set up a dinner date at his house. He invited Jesus and a large number of his friends and former business associates to the meal. At least, that is the way we would describe them. But Matthew doesn't. He comes right out and calls them as they are - tax collectors and sinners. They are people who don't measure up and are on the wrong side of God's law, (Matthew 9:10) and Matthew has invited them to meet his new friend Jesus. It's friend of a friend in action.

But the religious leaders didn't like it. It was not appropriate in their view. Eating in a house filled with sinners is not the place for someone like Jesus. But they were wrong. He was exactly where he needed to be. "It is not the healthy who need a doctor, but the sick." (Matthew 9:12) Jesus was the perfect fit for sinners. He was the powerful, rescuing friend they sorely needed. They weren't an unnecessary or unhelpful distraction for him. They were the very centre of what he had come to do. (Matthew 9:12-13)

At this point, I want to say that Jesus spent time with sinners because he loved them (which he did), but I hesitate. I hesitate because in some Christian circles, our understanding of love has been boiled down to the decisions or choices we make for the good of another person. And while this is a key part of what love is, it goes well beyond that. Genuine love involves affection. You can't truly love the other person if you don't like them. I think Jesus spent time with sinners because he liked them and enjoyed being with them. Do you think he would get the reputation as a 'friend of sinners' if he was preachy and standoffish and merely tolerating them? I don't think so either.

A little while ago, I had the opportunity to do some intensive ministry in a rehab centre. I was excited about the opportunity but had some concerns about how it would go because I had spent my whole life in the church and didn't have much experience with high end pastoral issues. I wondered how the gospel would connect to the residents' big problems. But I shouldn't have been concerned. The gospel of course came into its own in that environment. It was an amazing time.

Something else surprised me too – the honesty of the residents was like a cold drink of water on a hot day. I coined a term while I was there: authentically fallen. This is what they were. Their struggles were on the record, and they were honest about the mess they had made of their lives. There was no ducking or weaving, and no hiding from what their true problems were.

The longer I worked with the residents in the rehab

## Jesus Enjoys Sinners

centre, the more I realised how tricky and tiring it was to work with religious people who didn't think they had any problems. It was such a contrast. It gave me some insight into the way Jesus seemed to enjoy being with sinners.

Messy, broken sinners were and are Jesus' sweet spot. He didn't just hang out with them because he had to, I think he spent time with them because he wanted to. Those with broken and messy hearts, (Psalm 51:17) who are contrite and lowly, (Isaiah 57:15) seem to be his kind of people. In spite of the wreckage of their lives, Jesus seemed to be able to see through the debris to the person he had made them to be. Look at Jesus through these lenses and you won't be surprised to find him spending a lot of time with sinners.

But it isn't just about the sinners out there. It's about all of us. Is your life messy and you know it? Do your failures loom large? Does your backstory make you eligible for a dinner invitation to Matthew the tax collector's house? Do you think Jesus would come to your house for dinner if you invited him? I think he would. Every. Single. Time. And he wouldn't be sitting there watching the clock, waiting for the appropriate moment to go home. If he came to your house and you were honest and upfront about your failures, then he would enjoy being with you and interacting with you. He would stay with you until it was late. How do I know? Because he made his home in you when you became a Christian. Your mess doesn't put him off.

It appears the sinners enjoyed being with Jesus as well. They seemed to like eating and drinking with him and probably stayed late into the night too. They weren't forced to do it. They had the freedom to come and go as they pleased. But they stayed, and as they did, Jesus engaged in conversation with them.

I often wonder what Jesus and the sinners talked about. What we have in the gospels are snippets and summaries of the conversations they had, conversations which no doubt lasted much longer than what we read. From what we know, I don't think Jesus was preachy, nor would he have engaged in relentless bible bashing. That is not what friendship is about. Friendship is a two-way street. Friends engage in two-way conversations, not one-way monologues. He didn't hang out with sinners in a hall behind a lectern but in a home over dinner.

Jesus was obviously very skilled in engaging with people. When you remember how Jesus lived for 30 years before he began his ministry, how he was invited to a wedding in Cana before his ministry started, (John 2:1-12) and how children loved him, (Matthew 19:14) it makes me think he was an engaging and enjoyable person to be around. He just can't have been a religious grinch. Have you ever met a religious person who is having fun? Even innocent fun? That's my point. If you lived in Jesus' day, you would have liked to be with him, and he would have liked being with you.

## ENJOYING ONE ANOTHER

The Christian tradition I grew up in didn't leave very much space for enjoying sinners. We had a well-developed theology of sin; people were totally depraved, and their whole life had been affected. We were well-tuned into those realities. But what we failed to pay enough attention to was the residual image of God left in humanity after the fall. (Genesis 9:6) You see, it doesn't matter who it is, Christian or non-Christian, in their fallen state everyone still retains traces of who God made them to be. We still bear the resemblance of the one who made us in his image, (Genesis 1:27) and as his creatures we continue to display his invisible attributes. (Romans 1:20) Look past the rubble of what sin has done to humanity and you will see the remnants of the person God originally made them to be, remnants which point us to God himself. There is much of God to see in the people we mix with.

When I look at people around me and the incredible diversity in their personalities and talents, it makes me think about how talented God is and how diverse his personality must be. There are people like bookkeepers and jewellers who love to work with fine details, people who always have a cheeky look in their eye and something funny to say, those who can sing, those who are fiercely loyal, and those who keep soldiering on under the most immense pressure. I enjoy all of them and more.

There is so much to enjoy about who God has made people to be, but you need to slow down to see it. We tend to live our lives too fast. We run from one thing to another and are often over-stimulated, at the expense of actually seeing what is really there. We scroll and multitask with an insatiable desire for the next interesting thing, even as we walk straight past some of the most amazing people God has made, people who speak volumes about him. Have you ever slowed down enough to appreciate how wonderful it is that a mere facial expression or tone in a laugh can convey the most detailed of meanings in a fraction of a second? Our lack of enjoyment of others has more to do with us than we often realise.

Enjoyment of others is a huge part of what friendship is. If you don't enjoy other people, then it is going to be pretty hard to be friends with them. I understand there are times where it is hard to find something to enjoy in others. I have those times too. But don't give in. There is always something in other people that will remind you of God if you look closely enough. He is the one who is supremely enjoyable and there are countless ways humanity reflects his nature and images him.

The opportunity lies before us to see glimpses of God in and through our friends The moment we begin to do this will be the moment we discover that our enjoyment of others is at its core an enjoyment of our Creator. And as we enjoy other people more, we will inevitably find our enjoyment of them will spill over into a desire to see them come to Jesus.

## A CONVERSATION BETWEEN FRIENDS

At the end of my street, there are three sporting fields. About 2-3 times a week I head down there to jog for about half an hour. Sometimes people from my neighbourhood come down and walk their dogs there too.

## Jesus Enjoys Sinners

One of them is David, or Dave[2] as he is known. He isn't a Christian – or not yet anyway. I really enjoy Dave. He is probably in his mid-50s and is a very down to earth, blue-collar kind of guy. He is a high school woodwork teacher (something I used to do) and he works at a public school in the town in which I live.

Dave has knee troubles, and his ageing dog has arthritis in its hip. They both walk slowly with a limp. They are a pigeon pair. Who said dogs don't look like their owners? He is a real character too.

I always stop running when I catch up to where Dave is on the ovals. We stop and we talk. We talk about work, we talk about life, and we sometimes talk about God. He is an honest, genuine, hard-working man, who underneath it all wants the best for his wife and his children. I always enjoy catching up with him.

The other day we caught up on the oval as per usual, and he told me about his son who had just returned from a school trip to a country overseas with a vastly different culture to ours. Dave told me about how eye opening it was for him. I agreed with him and told him about how our church's missions trips had the same effect on our children as well. We covered a lot of territory in a short conversation. He talked about how that country's culture contrasted with Australian culture, then I talked about how Nepal contrasted with Australia and the differences between Hinduism (a central religious and cultural dynamic for Nepalis) and Jesus.

It wasn't weird, it wasn't forced, it wasn't about completing a task, and it wasn't about having something to share about an evangelism opportunity at my next small group meeting. It didn't end in Dave's conversion. It was just a conversation between friends.

> This is what the high and exalted One says— he who lives forever, whose name is holy: "I live in a high and holy place, but also with the one who is contrite and lowly in spirit, to revive the spirit of the lowly and to revive the heart of the contrite."
>
> Isaiah 57:15

## FOR REFLECTION AND DISCUSSION

1) What do you enjoy about other people? How does it remind you of God?

2) Who enjoys you? Why do you think they enjoy you?

3) Do you think Jesus enjoys you? Why/why not?

# 4

# Jesus Walks with Sinners

When my children were younger and we were walking somewhere, they developed a bad habit of walking behind me. It didn't matter whether we were walking to school or walking at the shops, they would often lag behind. It wasn't because I was walking too fast or they were in trouble, it was just a pattern they got into.

The first time it happened I didn't say anything about it. I thought it was probably a once off. But then it happened again and again, so I decided I would do something about it. The next time one of my sons dropped behind, I turned around and said, "Come up here and walk next to me. You're my son, not my dog." He got the idea. He hurried up next to me, and we began to walk together. "That's better," I thought. We are father and son. Fathers and sons walk together.

*Friends walk together too.*

The physical act of walking together is a wonderful picture of the most fundamental dynamic of friendship:

friends walk together, they do life together. While the depth in which people walk together varies from one friendship to another, friends are side by side. They travel through the highs and lows of life together.

## JESUS WALKED WITH HUMANITY

The metaphor of walking together is common in scripture. (Genesis 3:8, 5:24, Amos 3:3, John 6:66, 1 John 2:6) And just like the conventional usage of the phrase, it captures how we live our lives and who we do it with.

The first time it shows up in the bible is thick with irony. Adam and Eve, the pinnacle of God's creation, were in the Garden of Eden, an amazing place where everything flourished in the richness of his presence. But on one fateful day, a serpent slipped in and sold the lie to Adam and Eve that God was holding out on them, and they would be better off going it alone. They swallowed it hook, line and sinker, and the results were catastrophic. Their world began crashing down before their very eyes. (Genesis 3)

And in the middle of this unfolding catastrophe, we discover God is taking a walk in the Garden in the cool of the day. What a stunning contrast. At the time of the day when the cool breezes were blowing, God was taking a walk in the Garden. The implication seems to be that this was a normal occurrence for Adam and Eve - they should have been walking with him. But they weren't. They were busy looking for a place to hide. (Genesis 3:8) They had swallowed the lie that it is better to go it alone and were now living out the consequences of their choice.

But despite the dramatic relational dislocation which humanity's sin had brought about, scripture tells us God was not done walking with his people. Walking with humanity is an integral part of who God is - despite how tricky it tends to be. As history would show, some people returned the favour and made it clear that they wanted to walk with him, but most of the time humanity decided to go it alone.

Eventually the day came when God took on human flesh and walked with humanity in a way which no one ever dreamed he would. He came and did life together with us, with skin on! It was simply stunning. On the night before he was crucified, at the evening meal with his disciples, he went even further when he said, "I no longer call you servants ... Instead, I have called you friends." (John 15:15) You have to slow down and take that in. The God of the universe, the creator of everything, the one who commands the hosts of heaven, took on human flesh, hung out with humanity, and then called us his friends. And he didn't do it because he needed more friends – he had the perfect community of the Trinity after all. He did it because he knows at the core of his being that going it alone is never as good as being together.

Take a look at the gospels and you will see this dynamic playing out over and over again. There were so many opportunities and so many reasons why Jesus could have split off and gone it alone. I mean, the headaches associated with being connected to fallen humanity would be enough for most of us to choose that option. But he doesn't. Because there is something more important to him than getting jobs done and ticking tasks off a list, and that is being together. From his point of view, it is always better together.

While technology provides some opportunities to walk with other people virtually, nothing beats having "boots on the ground." This is a saying I often use at our church to describe the missional partnership we have with churches in Nepal. I have travelled to Nepal three times in the last two years out of a desire to walk together with our spiritual brothers and sisters in that country. Walking together is about personal proximity. Technology can help, but it can only get you so far. In the end, if you want to walk with others, nothing beats physical proximity - you need to have boots on the ground.

Jesus had boots on the ground when it came to walking with humanity. The incarnation is the only evidence you need. But his heart to walk with us, his boots on the ground approach, goes much further than that. If you want to see Jesus' heart to walk with humanity, then go to the gospels and locate all of the places where he is physically close to people. Those are the times where he is walking with humanity.

One of the first places you see this is the calling of twelve men to be his disciples. While he walked with many others, these were the ones who he committed to walk with ongoingly. They ate together, did ministry together, faced opposition together, and literally walked

## Jesus Walks with Sinners

and talked together. They did life together. When they were afraid, Jesus was with them to calm their fears. When they doubted, he challenged their doubts with the truth. When they felt powerless, he was there to strengthen them. When they were disoriented, he was there to stabilise them. Jesus walked with them.

The gospel of Luke tells the story of two followers of Jesus who were walking and talking together on the way to a village called Emmaus. It was shortly after the death and resurrection of Jesus. The topic of conversation was a blend of what they had seen happen to Jesus and the hopelessness and discouragement they felt as a result of it all. Partway through this conversation, "Jesus himself came up and walked along with them." (Luke 24:15) This is classic Jesus. Two people's heads are spinning and Jesus can help, so he comes alongside them and walks with them with a view to clearing up their confusion.

Jesus walked with many other people too, even if it was only for a limited time. He was personally close to anyone who came to him for help. Some needed healing, some needed deliverance, others came to get help for those they loved. It didn't seem to matter what they needed, Jesus was up-close-and-personal with them. There are only three healings in the gospels which are done remotely; the rest were done in person, often with a physical touch. Here is one of the reports in the gospels about how Jesus helped people:

## FRIEND OF A FRIEND

> Now when the sun was setting, all those who had any who were sick with various diseases brought them to him, and he laid his hands on every one of them and healed them.
>
> Luke 4:40

No one could accuse Jesus of being detached. That simply wasn't how he rolled. He was with people and walked with them as much as he could. No one got fobbed off and no one who came to him missed out. He never referred people to someone else. He didn't let their calls go through to voicemail. People got to be up close and personal with him. They got to touch him, and he touched them. They had space to tell him of their troubles and he helped them until there were none left. If you were there, he would have made space for you too.

People in my church have often asked me, "How much of my life does Jesus need to be part of?" And I say, "Just everything." No one is a face in the crowd to Jesus. He knows everyone's name and wants to be in on everything. He wants to walk with you all the time. Sometimes our shame can lead us into thinking he prefers to keep us at arm's length, and he wants to walk with other people but not us. But don't believe it. He took your specific sins to the cross, called you by name, and wants in on every part of your life. I assure you, his desire to walk with us is far stronger than our desire to walk with him.

## WALKING WITH OTHERS

The example of Jesus, and the metaphor of walking together, provide us with some helpful pointers when it comes to doing friendship with others. Here are four:

1) Walking together is invitational by nature – especially at the beginning. You can't force someone to begin walking with you physically, and you can't make someone continue to if they don't want to. It is the same in a relational sense. You can't make someone else walk through life with you. It is voluntary by nature. All you can do is invite others to walk with you and offer to walk with them. Forcing or manipulating someone to do life with you will only mangle the relationship and end up pushing people away.

   Here are some practical ways you can tell someone is inviting you to walk with them:

   - They speak about personal things to you
   - They ask you what you think about something
   - They are openly wondering

   Here are some practical ways you can let someone know you would like to walk with them:

   - Ask them questions about things they have said
   - Remember things they have said in the past and ask follow-up questions about them when you see them next
   - Identify with any pain or difficulty they tell you about

2) Walking together requires ongoing continuous agreement. (Amos 3:3) You may not notice it or even think about it, but you can't continue to walk with someone unless you both continuously agree to do so. It is rarely a verbal agreement, and almost never a written agreement, but it is an ongoing agreement nonetheless. For friendship to continue to grow, two people need to voluntarily and ongoingly agree to walk through life together. It simply won't happen if they don't agree to. If one person decides they don't want to walk together anymore or walk together any more deeply, then it won't happen. Jesus offered to walk with people who agreed to walk with him (Luke 24:13-35) and with those who declined his offer. (Matthew 19:21-22) When people didn't want to walk with him, Jesus always respected their choice. Walking together requires ongoing continuous agreement.

3) Walking together is side by side. There is no hierarchy in friendship. Although circumstances will arise from time to time where your friend has some expertise you need, or you have some expertise they need, friendship is not one-sided. Friendship is a two-way street. One moment, one person will be the expert, and the next moment the other person will be.

Any relationship where one person is ongoingly the giver and the other is always the receiver is probably not a friendship relationship. While Jesus is overwhelmingly the giver and expert in his friendships in the gospels, he still asked for help from others from time to time. The night before the crucifixion in the Garden of Gethsemane is one of these. (Matthew 26:38)

I experienced this dynamic of mutuality in one of my friendships this morning. I had been struggling with some of the content for this book and called my friend to let him know I needed his help. But before I could say anything, he jumped in. He needed to talk about something he was struggling with. He needed some help. And so, I pushed my needs aside so I could understand what was going on for him and provide some support and help. But before we were done, he asked me how I was going, and I had the opportunity to tell him about the writing struggles I was having. At that point we switched. He became the helper, and I became the one who was being helped. In friendships between people, there are no professionals. No one is the resident expert. Friendship is side by side.

4) Walking together is a long-term way of doing life not an objective to achieve. It is something which you do day by day, month by month, and year by year. You keep turning up. It is something you do at the same time as you are doing everything else. Friends walk together through the ups and downs of life. The biblical term which captures this dynamic

is 'faithful'. As the Proverb says, "Many claim to have unfailing love, but a faithful person who can find?" (Proverbs 20:6) We want to be faithful friends to others, like Jesus was a faithful friend to us. And because, well, there aren't very many of them.

Here is a good summary statement when it comes to friendship – it is better together. Always. It is the centre of what walking together is all about. If you get your head around this and you believe it at the core of your being, then you probably won't need most of the suggestions I just gave you. You will find yourself being personally close to others without even thinking about it.

## A FINAL HEADS-UP

While I want to encourage you to be friends with non-Christians and to walk through life with them, I do want you to be aware if you aren't already, about the fundamental disconnect you will encounter between the way you do life and the way they do. This disconnect ultimately comes down to a difference in what drives us. You need to know that you will make different decisions to them because you have something, or should I say someone, different in the centre of your life than they do.

As Christians, when it comes to our friendships, our first allegiance is to Jesus and his people, and then to others around us. Although this priority seems to relegate our other friendships to a lower level of importance, it will actually make us better friends in the end. As we do friendship with Jesus, he teaches us how to be a friend of his and how to be a friend of others – including those who don't know him.

## A CONVERSATION BETWEEN FRIENDS

One of the ways you can communicate your willingness to walk with your friends is by offering to help them when they are in need. Another way is by asking them for help when you are in need. Most of us find it harder to ask for help than we do to offer it. Here's a story which captures the power of asking someone for help.

I used to have a next-door neighbour called Col. He was a very private man, a retired military man, and he was outstanding at anything mechanical. We often enjoyed chatting and would regularly do so at the end of our street. A little while ago we arrived home from holidays late at night with a full car and camper trailer in tow. We had come home through a hilly rainforest area and were exhausted, so we took all of our perishables out of the car, put them in the fridge, and jumped straight into bed. In the morning I came out to discover one of the wheel bearings in our trailer had blown and we had only been millimetres away from the wheel falling off at high speed the night before.

I went straight across the road to Col and said, "Col. I need your help. Can you come and have a look at something. I'm not sure what to do." He came over, looked at the wheel, and said, "#!?*. That's not good at all, mate! Bring it over and I'll help you fix it." I took it to his place and over the next few hours he told me what to do, and I fixed the trailer. As I worked on it we talked about all sorts of things: church, family, and God, to name a few. My asking for help seemed to change the way we talked after that. Our relationship became more personal.

It wasn't anything mind-blowing, just a request for help and a subsequent conversation between friends.

> Now that same day two of them were going to a village called Emmaus, about seven miles from Jerusalem. They were talking with each other about everything that had happened. As they talked and discussed these things with each other, Jesus himself came up and walked along with them.
>
> Luke 24:13–15

### FOR REFLECTION AND DISCUSSION

1) Who do you do life with? What does it practically look like to walk with them?

2) What is one thing you can do this week to walk with someone who is not a Christian yet?

3) In what area of your life do you suspect God is wanting to walk more closely with you?

# 5

# Jesus Welcomes Interruptions by Sinners

In 2023, Chinese mountain climber Fan Jiangtao was only 400 metres from the summit of Mt Everest when he came upon a female climber who was shivering uncontrollably, out of oxygen, missing a glove and had a hand blackened by frostbite.[3] He was on a mission to reach the top of Everest, something which was his life's goal, and she was stuck. Left to herself, death was inevitable.

Mountaineers climbing Everest normally prioritise their mission to reach the summit rather than assist those in trouble, because it is extremely dangerous to help those who are stranded. But not Fan. He couldn't go on. He had to help her. His guide asked him many times about his decision to abandon ascending the summit. He replied, "Yes, my goal is to save a life." He stopped with the woman, refilled her oxygen with his, and worked to bring her back to consciousness.

But before long, Fan and his guide became too exhausted to help anymore. Fan went looking for someone to assist and found another Chinese climber Xie Ruxiang. Fan told Xie he wanted to save a life, but he was too exhausted and didn't have enough strength. Like Fan, Xie also chose to abandon his goal and joined in the rescue of the woman.

After the successful rescue the men reflected on the decision they had made. "Although we didn't reach the summit, saving a person's life is far more valuable than reaching the peak," Fan said. Xie added, "Ascending to the top of Everest is our dream, but it can't be compared with life."

They had almost completed their mission to climb the highest mountain in the world and were interrupted by a dying woman. They had a choice: press on and achieve what they had come to do, or give up the 'life' of ascending the summit so the woman could keep hers. It seems they didn't think twice about it.

Despite not knowing the woman, Fan and Xie were friends to her of the highest calibre. They did at a very high level (no pun intended) what all friends do a thousand times a year in a thousand different ways … mostly without thinking about it. They welcomed the interruption which the other person's need had brought into their lives, and they prioritised giving life over getting and retaining it for themselves.

Giving life to your friends isn't a big deal most of the time. Your friend messages you and you can tell they are not doing well, so you take a couple of moments to compose an encouraging reply or you call them. You find out your friend is sick and unable to get one of their children to sports training, so you give up your time and a little fuel in your car to help them out. You hear there is sickness in your friend's family or extended family, and you make a meal for them or organise to have food delivered to them. Sometimes friendship is about big moments, but most of the time it isn't. Most of the time it is about small ones.

## JESUS IS VERY INTERRUPTIBLE

If being interruptible for the sake of giving life to another person is one of the marks of friendship, then Jesus was an incredible friend. There is no doubt about it. You only need to set aside an afternoon to read the four gospels, paying special attention to the number of times Jesus gets interrupted to see this. The frequency with which it happens will surprise you. It surprised me. It wasn't long before I began wondering when he would lose his cool with someone. But he never does. Oh, except for demons and religious people bent on stopping the good things he was doing. (Mark 1:25, 3:5) But that's a different story.

Every time someone came to Jesus for help, they received it. Every time someone was tangled in the cords of death in one way or another, he worked to free them. Like a true friend, whenever someone was in need and asked for his help, his answer was always yes.

One of those times occurred in the gospel of Mark when Jesus was in Capernaum preaching to a large crowd in a house. (Mark 2:1-12, also Luke 5:17-26) The crowd had filled the house and was spilling outside of it.

As he was preaching, four men arrived carrying a paralysed man. Their mission was clear: they needed to get their friend to Jesus. It didn't matter to them that Jesus was in the middle of something important, they had to get their friend to him.

The size of the crowd meant conventional means would not do. No one was going to be able to get a man on a stretcher into that house with all those people in there. So they went onto the roof, removed some tiles, and lowered their friend down right in front of Jesus as he preached. It would have been quite an entrance. They were interrupting Jesus with the man's need. What happened next is classic Jesus – he gave the man more grace than he came for. By the end of the scene the man is healed *and* forgiven. What a sublime combination of words. You will hear those words one day, and it will be the sweetest day of all.

Other times, Jesus is interrupted on his way somewhere. One of the more well-known examples of this is the healing of blind Bartimaeus. (Mark 10:46-52) Bartimaeus was sitting by the roadside begging as Jesus left Jericho one day. Somehow he found out Jesus was passing by, and he called out to him for mercy. But Bartimaeus' cry was not welcomed by anyone around him. They told him to be quiet. They didn't want him to interrupt what was going on. But he didn't care. He was in need, and he knew Jesus could help, so he shouted out even louder. Jesus stopped, called for the man to come to him, and after a short conversation, healed the man's eyes. The death which had darkened the man's eyes was

## Jesus Welcomes Interruptions by Sinners

reversed. He could see again, and he began to follow Jesus. We never hear of him again in scripture or in the early church. But it doesn't matter. What mattered is that he mattered to Jesus.

Time doesn't permit me to talk about every person who interrupted Jesus. There was the woman with the flow of blood who touched Jesus when he was on the way to help Jairus' daughter, (Mark 5:21-43) the disciples who woke him up in the storm on the sea of Galilee, (Mark 4:35-41) the massive crowd who interrupted him and his disciples when they were desperate for some down time, (Matthew 14:1-14) the widow of Nain on the way to bury her only son, (Luke 7:11-17) and so many more. Each time Jesus willingly set aside what he was doing in order to give life to those in the grip of death. It's what he does.

With Jesus, interruptions aren't a hassle or an irritation. He welcomes them as an opportunity to give life to others – something true friends do. Sometimes I hear people talk about areas in their life which they haven't prayed about because they think Jesus is too busy or he has more important things to deal with. But they are wrong. Jesus is not bound by the limitations of human friends. He is a mighty friend. If you have ever thought these things then you need to know Jesus never sees your requests as an unwelcome interruption, but as an opportunity to do good and bring life to you. He is a true friend.

## THE PUREST LIFE

The way healthy friendships work is a reminder that the purest form of life is life which is given and received, not taken. It stands in stark contrast to our fallen human tendency to snatch and grasp after more life – something which seems to be woven into our DNA. It is a tendency which can be traced right back to the lie peddled by the serpent in the Garden of Eden. Built into it was the idea that the best life is the life you need to take for yourself, not life which is given to you. (Genesis 3:5) But it was wrong, dead wrong. Adam and Eve fell for it, and we have followed in their footsteps.

But friendships, all true friendships, run to a different tune. They don't run on taking or grasping after life, they thrive and flourish on giving and receiving it. Jesus taught the disciples about this friendship dynamic the night before he died on the cross, "Greater love has no one than this: to lay down one's life for one's friends." (John 15:13) The reason there is no greater love for another than laying down your life is because there is nothing of more value to someone than their own life. If they give up their life for their friend then it proves their friend is more valuable to them than the most valuable thing they own.

While literally giving up your life for another is the ultimate act of love, laying down your life for your friends is not limited to this. If it was then we would only be able to do it once. Laying down your life is something friends do in countless small ways every day. The apostle

John made this clear in his application of Jesus' teaching, "This is how we know what love is: Jesus Christ laid down his life for us. And we ought to lay down our lives for our brothers and sisters." (1 John 3:16) John isn't talking about actually dying for someone else, he is talking about all of the small moments every day where we forego what life we could have in order to give it to others. It is the heart and soul of friendship. All true friendships live and thrive on the countless times where friends forego what they want for the sake of giving life to their friend.

At this point, I could nail down a long list of bullet points which describe all of the ways you should be putting others before yourself. But I won't. At least not this time anyway. Because I don't want you to turn loving others into a task. Instead, I want to say to you, "Be a good friend. Take notice when things are not going well for your friends and do what you can to give life to them." Friendship is the mega category under which laying down your life falls. The more you think about being a good friend the less you will think about love as a to do list.

## INTERRUPTIBILITY

Whether the Chinese climbers knew Jesus or not, they reflected him in the way they laid down their lives for the woman who was dying. Their sacrifice for the woman had a gospel shape to it – a shape which is found in all true friendships. One person foregoes life, they embrace death, in order to give life to their friend.

For friends, this decision is not normally a long, drawn-out decision. It's typically a quick, mostly automatic, reflex action, or instinctive reaction. They see death at work in their friend and they do what they can to give life to them.

But sometimes it doesn't happen. Sometimes other things get in the way and make a straightforward decision much more complicated. It seems interruptibility, a key ingredient of friendship, can itself be interrupted. Busyness can do it, and so can our wants and desires.

Let's start with busyness. While there are some exceptions, there are many of us who are so busy we don't have time for any interruptions. We have added more and more things to our schedule until there is no margin left for anything else. This has left us in a place where we run from one thing to another, sometimes for months, without seeing or engaging personally with anyone who doesn't know Jesus. It's tragic to admit it, but if we are honest we have to admit we are so busy sometimes that we don't notice those around us who are in the grip of death. It's as though they are in the grip of a python which has trapped them and is squeezing the life out of them, and we are going too fast to see it. If we are to be good friends to others, then we will need to slow down, hold our plans loosely, and make sure we have enough margin to be interrupted when the need arises.

Our interruptibility is also interrupted when we fall for the same lie Adam and Eve fell for in the Garden. All of us know what it is like to want something too much. One would have thought we would be able to see through it by now. But human history and our own lived experience is the only evidence needed to prove we haven't. The battle is real. Our problem is not that we have desires, it's that our desires get too big, and they begin to rule us. And when they do, we become obsessed with getting life for ourselves and no room is left for anyone else – even our friends. In these moments, what we need to do is turn away from our desires and turn back to Jesus. We need to remember the best life, life which is the most satisfying, life with the greatest staying power, is life which is freely given and received, not life which you snatch for or grasp after.

Before we finish this chapter, I want to clarify something. It is an important clarification because we are living in the most interrupted era in human history. So many things compete for our attention – the notifications on our phones, all-pervasive marketing, the 24/7 news cycle, and the FOMO (fear of missing out) of social media. All of these and more interrupt us and bleat for our attention. While in one sense you could argue we are more interruptible than ever, this is not the kind of interruptibility I am encouraging you to grow in.

The kind of interruptibility I am keen for us to grow in is an interruptibility which is calibrated in favour of the most personal of interruptions. Most of the interruptions in our culture are impersonal. What we want to be doing is tuning in more closely to what will make us more personal and more relational, not less. I invite you to join me in cultivating a bias in our lives which leans away from ourselves and what we are doing, and towards others around us and what is happening for them. In my view, these are the best kinds of interruptions.

## A CONVERSATION BETWEEN FRIENDS

It was late in the afternoon, and I was on my way home. It had been a long hot summer's day teaching high school students and the only thing between me and the refuge of our home's air-conditioning was a short walk. I was dressed in my normal teaching attire: long pants, tie, long sleeve shirt, and a large backpack. As a high school woodwork teacher, whatever part of me which was not covered by clothing was a sticky mixture of sawdust and perspiration.

We lived next door to the school and the quickest route home was to cut across a vacant block. As I walked across, I noticed my next door neighbour Darrell standing behind his car. There had been some major flash flooding in our city, and he had just arrived home from the funeral of a mother and daughter who had lost their lives in the floods.

I wanted to get home. I wanted to take a shower, have a cold drink, catch up with my wife and kids, and sit down for a moment. I wanted more life; it was so close. But Darrell had been facing death all afternoon and he was my friend, so I veered across to him and asked about the funeral and how he was going. He still recalls me coming across on that hot afternoon with my backpack on.

He told me it was a horrible afternoon. He wasn't a Christian at this point, and he didn't have many categories for orienting himself in the midst of that kind of tragedy. He talked, I listened, and walked alongside him like any friend would. By the time we were done, we had talked all things life and death, including eternity and God himself.

While I eventually made it home, I never regretted stopping for that conversation. Neither did Darrell. To this day, he says it was *the* moment where he started thinking about God and taking him seriously. According to him, the most impacting part of it wasn't anything I said, it was my going across to see him.

Sometime after this, Darrell came up to my place to get some help with things which were happening in his family. He needed to talk, and I was more than happy to listen. At the end of our conversation, I asked him if he would mind if I prayed for him. He said, "Yes please." At the end of the prayer, I opened my eyes and tears were streaming down his face. As we reflected on these things a couple of weeks ago, I asked him why he became emotional. He said, "When someone prays for you, it's gotta mean something." He went on and explained how the combination of a caring friend and coming to God in prayer had moved him deeply. A short time later, Darrell started attending our church, and before long we baptised him.

Darrell and his family continue to be close friends of ours. What I did wasn't revolutionary. It's what friends do. Friends welcome any opportunity to give life to one another.

Darrell wasn't an evangelism project or a missional

target, and our conversation wasn't a carefully crafted evangelistic moment which I was able to skilfully steer in a spiritual direction. It was just a conversation between friends.

> As Jesus approached the town gate, a dead person was being carried out—the only son of his mother, and she was a widow. And a large crowd from the town was with her. When the Lord saw her, his heart went out to her.
>
> Luke 7:12–13

## FOR REFLECTION AND DISCUSSION

1) Who is in the grip of death around you? What could you do to give them life?

2) Which enemy of interruptibility is more powerful in your life: wants and desires or busyness?

3) When was the last time someone gave some of their life to you? What did it mean to you?

# 6

# Jesus is Personal with Sinners

I just watched a confession from someone on social media. They had posted a video where they told the world about how who they seemed to be on the outside, the person they told everyone they were, was not the person they really are. You've probably seen one of these. They seem to be a somewhat regular feature.

They had previously projected a version of themselves where they had all the money, the toys, the family, and business success anyone could ever want. But on the inside, they were messed up. In their latest post, they spoke of trauma, drug addiction, marital problems, and a recent stint in rehab. I didn't quite know how to feel. I was glad they were being honest, but I couldn't snuff the thought out of my mind that this too was another projection - a seemingly constant danger for anyone wanting to be personal on social media.

As I thought about it some more, I realised the contours of their story are not much different to ours. While you and I may not have many things in common with the details of their life, we can identify with the tendency to project a version of ourselves to others which is different to who we truly are underneath. These kinds of moments remind us that what people can see of us using their eyes is only a small portion of who we really are.

## BEING PERSONAL

There are two parts to every person – a physical and a non-physical part. The physical part of who we are has to do with our height, weight, the shape of our nose, our skin colour and so on. Although it is an important part, this visible part of us is not the main part of who we are. Most of who we are is invisible. It involves the way we think, our will, our emotions, our likes and dislikes, our passions, giftings, strengths and weaknesses and so on. It is the part of us which other people need to see and know if we are to engage in relationships or friendships with them.

The mechanism by which we allow ourselves to be known by others is captured by the phrase self-revelation. Self-revelation involves opening ourselves up to others so we can be known by them. A more street-level way of describing self-revelation is the word personal. When we refer to someone as saying or doing something personal, what we mean is that someone has said or done something which tells us about who they are underneath.

People operate personally when they act and speak in ways which communicate the invisible part of who they are. Operating personally is essential for forming and deepening friendships, because it is the means by which we know and are known by others – the engine room of relationships. It is the mechanism which makes knowing and being known go. (1 Corinthians 13:12) As people engage in being personal with one another in a progressively deepening way, friendships grow.

## JESUS IS PERSONAL

It comes as no surprise to us that the most personal and relational of all beings, God himself, operates personally by default. He is a self-revealer by nature and has operated personally since the creation of the world. Self-revelation or operating personally is a function of his personhood, an expression of his desire to be in relationship with humanity. He puts himself out there so we would know him personally and walk with him.

For the most part, we work out who God is from what he says and how he interacts with people in the biblical story. But there are moments where he is very clear and direct in what he communicates about himself. Moses' interaction with God on Sinai is a good example of this. "The LORD, the LORD, the compassionate and gracious God, slow to anger, abounding in love and faithfulness …" (Exodus 34:6)

What we have here in this story is God coming right out and telling Moses who he is. And while countless people have read it since, you need to pay close attention to the context to notice the beauty of it. You see, God wasn't revealing himself to 50, or 500, or 5 000 people. He was revealing himself to one person – the one who

God spoke to as a man speaks with his friend. (Exodus 33:11) And we get the privilege of eavesdropping on it.

While there are many amazing moments in the Old Testament where God revealed who he is, they are all but a shadow of the self-revelation which came in the incarnation of Jesus. (Hebrews 1:1-2) The apostle John spoke directly about this in the introduction to his gospel, "No one has ever seen God, but the one and only Son, who is himself God and is in closest relationship with the Father, has made him known." (John 1:18) Jesus is the ultimate self-revelation of God, in human flesh, sent to restore relationship with his estranged children.

Take a look at the way Jesus operates in the gospels, and you will see him being personal with just about everyone he comes into contact with. We see his emotions, hear about what he likes and dislikes, see his will in action, and so on. Whenever you notice him being personal with others, what you are observing is an invitation for others to know and be in relationship with him.

One of the most stunning times where Jesus operates personally was in the Garden of Gethsemane on the night before the crucifixion. (Matthew 26:36-46) The last supper was over, and he and his disciples had gone to the garden to pray. The weight of what was coming the next day was upon him. He wasn't just going to be executed, he was going to be executed and carry the sins of the world. No one else would ever do that.

It was a dark and difficult night for Jesus, but a night he could have handled with the help of the Father, the Holy Spirit, and the hosts of heaven who were on hand. He could have done it without the disciples, but he didn't. In one of his most difficult moments, he went to the garden with the twelve, and then took three of them further in with him. He was living out the truth at the centre of the universe. A truth which has stood for all time and flows directly from the trinity - it is better together.

He said to Peter, James and John, "My soul is overwhelmed with sorrow to the point of death. Stay here and keep watch with me." (Matthew 26:38) Did you notice what Jesus was doing here? He was being personal with them. While it is possible they could have picked something up about how he was going from his body language, or from what he had said that night, he didn't leave it to chance. He opened up his life to them and let them see who he was.

And it wasn't pretty. What Jesus was going through wasn't a minor irritation after being cut off by another driver, or a complaint about a dog biting him, or even that one of the religious leaders had tried to stop him from doing something good again. He is sorrowful to the point of death. And in this moment he took the opportunity to let the disciples in on the part of him which was hurting the most. Why? The last two words of the verse give it away - "with me." He felt the weight of the moment, and he wanted them to walk through it with him; he wanted to do it together.

We shouldn't be surprised at the way Jesus opened himself up to be known. He had been doing this all the way along. Being personal was what moved the disciples from being servants to friends in the first place. "I no longer call you servants, because a servant does not know his master's business. Instead, I have called you friends, for everything that I learned from my Father I have made known to you." (John 15:15) When they knew less, they were called servants and when they knew more, they were called friends. Now he is letting them into the deepest part of his life.

If we didn't know anything else about these three men, we could be forgiven for thinking it was easy for Jesus to let them in on what was happening for him. I mean, there was nothing in him which was messy or unpresentable like there is in us. In our fallenness, being known and not loved is a very real possibility. Understandably, it is one of our greatest fears. But Jesus was perfect, so he didn't have to deal with this fear, right? It would have been easy to let them know him, wouldn't it? Well, not really.

The possibility of being known and not loved was a very real risk for Jesus too, even though he was perfect. Anytime someone is personal and is treated with little or no value, they are known and not loved, and it hurts. It's not long after Jesus said this to the disciples that he finds them fast asleep. He put himself out there and he didn't matter enough to them to keep them awake. It wasn't the first time he had been known and not loved. He had experienced it throughout his life. But it didn't stop him being personal again. Jesus is intent on doing relationship with them, so he continues to open up his life to them even though he knows they will fall asleep, even though he knows Peter is about to betray him, and even in spite of a recent conversation with James' and John's mother about who was the greatest.

## TAKING THE PLUNGE

Despite the simplicity of knowing and being known and the rewards associated with it, the fear of being known and not loved is a powerful force which can quickly make our friendships terminally superficial. Unless we actively work against it, we will find ourselves engaging in small talk, frivolous joking, and conversations which never get below the surface, and end up in a place where we don't know each other at all. Some of these kinds of conversations can go on for decades, even a lifetime.

While the fear of being known and not loved can work against us, what runs in our favour is our built-in longing to be known by our friends. I am yet to meet someone who doesn't want to be truly known. It is the way we have been made. And herein lies most of our problem: we easily get stuck between the desire to be known and the fear of being known. It isn't a Christian problem, it is a human problem. We all struggle with it.

Progress is possible, but someone needs to break the deadlock. Someone needs to have the courage to take the lead in being personal. Someone needs to be the ice breaker. They don't need to share the deepest darkest secrets about their lives, they just need to share something, anything which matters to them which is connected to who they truly are. Once they do, others will jump in and be personal too. Here's how it usually works: The person who goes first stares down the fear of being known and not loved and operates personally. Their self-revelation creates a safe space where others discover they aren't weird, hideous, or a special case after all - a space where the other person's deep desire to be known can rise to the surface.

When it comes to having personal conversations with your non-Christian friends, here's my encouragement – be the first to take the plunge. You are the one who is best placed to do this. You have the king of the universe on your side, you have had your sins forgiven by Jesus, he knows you completely and he loves you anyway. You have less to risk and more security than those who don't know him yet, so jump in and let them know something personal about yourself. It doesn't have to be a heavy intense thing, just something personal to you. Put it out there and see what happens.

When we refuse to pretend we have all the answers or that we have it all sorted, it gives other people permission to be honest and transparent too. It also pushes back on the assumption that Christians are good people who have it all together. I have taken this approach for years and have frequently found myself in personal conversations with people who rarely speak on that level with others. It's not a special skill, it's just being honest, being vulnerable, and it is a key ingredient in healthy relationships and good conversations.

As you are personal with others, you will find your relationships with them will deepen and there will be more and more places where your friendship with Jesus will naturally fit into your conversations with them. But regardless of whether you get to talk about Jesus or not, every personal conversation is a win. He will come up eventually. You and your friend were made for him after all.

## OPERATING PERSONALLY

Let me get really practical and specific. If you don't know where to start when it comes to being personal, take a look at the list below which describes some of the non-physical elements of who you are.

- Will
- Likes/dislikes
- Passions
- Gifting
- Strengths/weaknesses
- Thinking
- Emotions

Stop and think about each of them for a moment. What categories above can you identify in your own life? Once you have done this, take a moment to think about some of the different aspects of who you are in each of these categories. Then rank them from those which are less personal to those which are more personal.

Start with less personal likes and dislikes such as your favourite colour, or favourite breed of dog, right up to more personal things such as how much you dislike the critical things people have said about you in the past. Or start with some of your less personal weaknesses such as how slow you run right through to more personal weaknesses such as the last time you blew it with your spouse or housemate.

Then, when the opportunity arises, share some of these things naturally in your conversations with other people. The wisest way to do this is to move from sharing less personal things to more personal things in response to the way your friend handles what you share. If they handle you well, go a step deeper, if they don't, then wait at that level until trust grows and you are able to go deeper. This process is the natural way friendships develop and deepen. As your friend demonstrates they are careful with what you have shared, then you can take the next step and entrust more of yourself to them. (John 2:24-25)

I have found that a good rule of thumb to guide how personal you are in the early stages of friendship is to only share things which won't deeply hurt you if the other person mishandles them. It is a principle which is especially important when you encounter people who regularly mishandle or hurt others.

### A CONVERSATION BETWEEN FRIENDS

I remember having a conversation with a non-Christian friend of mine as we watched our boys play rugby union one night. The game went for about an hour. It was a wide-ranging conversation which covered all sorts of topics such as work, family, and what we had planned for the rest of the year. As the conversation moved along, an opportunity came up for me to be honest about something in my life which I was anxious about.

I paused internally for a moment to consider whether I would share it with him or not. I did a quick risk analysis and decided that though the issue was bothering me, it wasn't going to be the end of the world for me if he mishandled my struggle. So, I told him. The whole conversation changed in that moment. He started telling me about things which he was anxious about, things which were troubling him. By the end of the conversation I had the opportunity to share how I handled my anxiety by trusting in Jesus.

It was a simple conversation, a conversation between friends – a conversation where I had the opportunity to talk about one of my other friends, Jesus.

> My soul is overwhelmed with sorrow to the point of death. Stay here and keep watch with me.
>
> Matthew 26:38

## FOR REFLECTION AND DISCUSSION

1) What makes you hesitate to be personal with others?

2) What is something personal you can tell one of your non-Christian friends which they don't already know about you?

3) What other examples can you think of in scripture where God is personal with humanity?

# 7

# Jesus Knows Sinners

I find people fascinating. I can sit and watch them for ages. Often on my day off, I will go to a cafe in our local shopping centre, read scripture, pray, and watch what people are up to. I sit and wonder why they are walking so fast, how they ended up with a scowl on their face, or where they just came from. I watch as people talk and react to one another and wonder what the topic of their conversation is.

My natural curiosity has served me well in the people-oriented work I do. It slows me down and it makes me pay attention to what is happening around me.

Curiosity is essential for healthy friendships too because of the way it helps us to be ready to learn about one another. People who are curious and inquisitive are learners by nature. Curious people ask lots of questions. The book of Proverbs makes a direct connection between curiosity and skilfulness in knowing who people truly are – "The purpose in a man's heart is like deep water, but a man of understanding will draw it out." (Proverbs 20:5)

For humanity, curiosity is an essential starting point in the relational process of knowing and being known.

## KNOWING SINNERS

The significance of curiosity in relationships makes us wonder if it was important for Jesus too. But when you remember how much Jesus knows, you quickly realise he has absolutely no need of it. He knows everything about everyone anyway. Why would he need to be curious? God knows everything in the past, the present, the future, and every possible thing which could happen. As fully man and fully God, Jesus shares this knowledge too – something frequently seen in the life of Jesus. (John 4:18, 13:38, 18:4)

But if Jesus has no need for curiosity, then why does he ask people questions? Is he just toying with them? Is he just pretending to not know something he already knows? Obviously there are times where Jesus asks questions as part and parcel of a truth he is teaching, but what about all the times where he asks people questions which he already knows the answer to? What about those?

You don't need to look very far in the gospels to find Jesus asking people these kinds of questions. One time a woman in a large crowd snuck in and touched Jesus' robe and was healed. Immediately after she had done it, Jesus turned around and asked, "Who touched me?" (Luke 8:45) Another time involved Bartimaeus, the blind beggar who cried out for mercy as Jesus walked past. Jesus asked him, "What do you want me to do for you?" (Mark 10:51) Or the time when Jesus arrived at Bethany after the death of Lazarus. When he got there he asked Mary and Martha where they had buried him. (John 11:34) Did Jesus know who touched him? Did he know what Bartimaeus wanted? Did he know where Lazarus was buried? Of course he did. Then what is he up to? Why does Jesus ask people questions which he knows the answer to?

Jesus asks people questions in order to know them personally. He does this because knowing about someone and knowing them are two different things. To know about someone is to know information or data, to know someone is to be in relationship with them. (Matthew 7:23) Knowing about someone is impersonal and distant, knowing someone is up close and personal.[4] Friends don't just know about each other. Friends know one another.

A key ingredient within this dynamic of knowing and being known by someone is knowing you are known by them. That is why conversations are such a critical part of knowing and being known. In healthy conversations, one person speaks while the other person listens. Then the listener asks a question or two to understand the speaker, who then clarifies what they are saying. And then, perhaps at some point, the listener summarises what the speaker has been saying, or they give a knowing nod, and it is met with hearty agreement. What is taking place in this simple process? The listener is engaging in the process of knowing their friend and the speaker is engaged in the experience of knowing they are known by them. This is what Jesus is engaging in when he asks people questions.

Take the man at the pool of Bethesda for example. (John 5:1-15) He had been an invalid for 38 years and was lying next to the pool in the hope he would be healed by touching the water when it was stirred. Jesus saw the man lying there and asked him, "Do you want to get well?" (John 5:6) What an obvious question to ask! You didn't need to be Jesus to know the answer to that one. Just about everyone at the pool was there for that reason. So, why did he ask it?

Looks can be deceiving. If you slow down and consider the nature of Jesus' question, you will notice how rich it is. With this simple question, Jesus invited the man to say something about himself. He invited him to be personal about his condition, to say something about what was going on underneath the surface.

What happens next is what often happens when people are given the opportunity to be personal – Jesus gets more than he asked for. The invalid doesn't waste time answering Jesus' yes/no question because everyone knows what the answer is. He seizes the chance to be more personal. "Sir ... I have no one to help me into the pool when the water is stirred. While I am trying to get in, someone else goes down ahead of me." (John 5:7) He isn't just an invalid; he is an invalid who is alone, stuck, and beaten to the punch. That's worse.

Jesus asked the man a personal question in order to engage in the relationally rich process of knowing and being known. Even though it was only for a moment, it

## Jesus Knows Sinners

was an opportunity for Jesus to be a friend to the man, an opportunity for the man to be known by him, and to know he was known by Jesus.

Jesus asks you this kind of question too. He wants to know what you like, what matters to you, what weighs you down, and what you enjoy. He wants to know you. His heart to know you is clear throughout scripture. His extensive knowledge of you is not meant to put you off praying. Rather, it is a powerful reason to pray. (Matthew 6:8-9) He wants you to talk to him and let him know what is going on for you. Engage in conversation with him. Listen to him as you read scripture and talk to him by telling him what is on your heart. While it won't be news to him, you will find yourself knowing you are known by him, and it will do wonders for your friendship.

### GOOD QUESTIONS

When it comes to knowing people, we have a little more work to do than Jesus. He knows everything about everyone before they open their mouths and only needs to engage in knowing and being known for the sake of doing relationship with them. We on the other hand, need to learn things about our friend which we don't know *and* engage in the process of doing relationship with them. But don't be discouraged, learning about others and doing relationship naturally fit together.

Start by firing up your curiosity. Don't begin by thinking mainly about what you do know, but about what you don't. Assume you don't understand or know things accurately and that there is a better more detailed explanation than you currently have. People who say, "I totally understand", too early in conversations, most of the time don't. Take the posture of a learner from the get-go and approach each conversation with a happy openness. It's the best place to start.

Then, once you are genuinely interested in others, your next step is to ask some good questions. They are the most effective tool for knowing others. Here are some different categories of questions which are a helpful part of everyday conversations between friends:

1) What? When? Where? How?

    These questions nail down some of the finer details and are essential in understanding what has happened. You can ask them whenever you need to but be careful you don't ask too many in a row. Doing this can make the conversation sound like an interrogation. Remember: when your friend is telling you about what happened to them, your main objective is to understand what it was like for them, not all of the minute details.

2) What do you mean by that?

    This kind of question is a critical part of most conversations. Language is often unclear. People can be using the same words and yet mean different things. Asking this question ensures that everyone in the conversation is talking about the same thing.

## Jesus Knows Sinners

3) Why?

This question can be helpful in ascertaining some of the reasons why something happened or why someone did what they did in a particular situation. It gets to the heart of why people acted the way they did. You can ask people 'why' directly, or you can ask any number of variations on it. Here are a couple of other ways to ask it:

- What were you trying to achieve by doing that?
- That doesn't seem to make sense to me. Can you help me out?

People's assessment of the reasoning behind an action or an event is a very rich source of information in understanding who they are and the way they see life. Just be aware that there will be times where people don't know the answer to this question. We don't always know why we do what we do either.

4) What was that like for you? What did it mean to you? I want to know about you in the middle of the situation.

In my view, this is the best category of question. I like this one the most because regardless of the event, regardless of whatever happened, I want to know what it was like for my friend in the middle of it. I want to know who they are, and I want to know how it affected them. In short, this type of question communicates that I want to know them. It is the category I want to get to the most because it is the place where two people get to walk together in the details of their lives.

## IMAGINATION

After you have asked a good question, engage your imagination. It will help you to understand and know the situation which your friend is describing to you. Whether you realise it or not, your imagination is employed much more frequently to see what is real rather than what isn't. In high school science I learnt how photosynthesis works. I learnt about the roots of a tree, the trunk, the leaves, the carbon dioxide going into them, and the oxygen being produced. When I look at a tree I can see this whole process, even though I can't. This is my imagination at work.

The same dynamic operates in our conversations with friends. As you listen to people, engage your imagination so you can 'see' what they are talking about. Don't spend your time thinking about the next thing you are going to say. Listen to what they are saying and try to picture it as they are describing it. Think about what they are like and try to imagine how they would have responded in the situation they are describing to you. Imagine how they would be feeling given what they have just told you. Imagine how you would respond if you were in the same situation.

*What is it like for them?*

*What would it be like if I was in the middle of that situation?*

*Why is it going on?*

If you are curious, if you ask good questions, and if you engage your imagination, then you will be well on the way to knowing your friend.

## A CONVERSATION BETWEEN FRIENDS

Trent dropped in to see me at church. He wasn't a Christian, but he had been to a couple of our services and had asked someone from the church to organise a meeting with me. He needed help and he figured I was his best option.

The moment for the meeting arrived. Trent walked into my office, we shook hands, introduced ourselves, and sat down. He was dishevelled, covered in tattoos, and was agitated and on edge. He avoided eye contact as much as possible.

We didn't engage in much small talk before I invited him to tell me a little of his back story and why he had wanted to come and see me. He jumped right in. Over the first half hour he told me about his messed up family, the death of his career dreams, the friends who had let him down, and the drugs he had been taking. His story was laced with expletives.

The more Trent talked the more I liked him. He didn't care what I thought, he was straight with me, and he didn't mince words. I didn't need to wade through religious jargon or clear away any false projection of himself. He was upfront, raw, and real. He was authentically fallen. I'm sure Jesus would have liked him too.

As he talked, he made one thing crystal clear – he didn't trust anyone. I could tell. People had hurt him, they had let him down, and he was on guard. No one else had protected him and it was up to him to look after himself. Everyone was a risk, no one was allowed to get close. But it wasn't working for him. Everything was getting on top of him. He was suicidal.

He came to me because I was a preacher, but he didn't need a preacher. He needed a friend. He needed someone to listen to him and know him. He needed someone who was interested in him.

So, I asked him questions and listened to his answers. In that moment being a pastor or preacher was the furthest thing from my mind. I just wanted to be a good friend. I wanted to know him, and for him to know he was known by me.

While the conversation was erratic at times, we ended up talking about Jesus. We were in a church after all. I didn't say very much. I just asked a few questions which were aimed at helping him to stay open to someone loving him sometime in the future – a dangerous option for him.

I said, "What if there was someone who could see you in all your mess, someone who wasn't in denial about what you have done or what has been done to you, and still loves you?"

He looked up and stared directly at me without saying a word.

## Jesus Knows Sinners

"Because there is someone like that. His name is Jesus."

He responded, "That's disgustingly alluring."

I will never forget the phrase. It was such an articulate and fitting way to put it. I knew exactly what he meant. These three words summed up his situation perfectly. We wrapped up the conversation and he left. I followed him up via his friend but I never heard from him again.

We weren't friends at the start, and we haven't seen each other since, but in that moment, what he needed most was someone who would take the time to know him. He needed a friend, a conversation with a friend.

> I no longer call you servants, because a servant does not know his master's business. Instead, I have called you friends, for everything that I learned from my Father I have made known to you.
>
> John 15:15

### FOR REFLECTION AND DISCUSSION

1) Who knows the real you?

2) How much do you think Jesus wants to know you? How interested is he really?

3) What are two or three questions you could begin asking others in order to know them better?

# 8

# Jesus Sees Sinners

One of the hidden gems in the Old Testament is the story of Hagar's conversation with God after fleeing from Sarai.

The back story to this conversation began with God's promise to Abram to make him into a great nation. He would eventually have offspring more numerous than the stars in the sky. But as time dragged on, Abram and Sarai continued to be childless. It just wasn't happening, and Sarai knew it. She laid the blame squarely at God's feet (Genesis 16:2) and she came up with an alternative plan. Her plan involved Abram sleeping with Hagar. He agreed. This is where things began to unravel.

Abram slept with Hagar, and she conceived. Shortly after, she began to despise Sarai. Sarai struggled with this and complained to Abram about it. He told her that she could do as she pleased with Hagar. And she did. Sarai treated Hagar harshly until she fled from her.

Hagar ended up isolated and alone, near a spring in the desert, with a child on the way. It was a mess. Sin, shame and trouble had done their dirty work again -

someone had to go. But she wasn't invisible to God. He saw her sitting there and he dropped in to have a chat with her. (Genesis 16:7,13) His opening question was, "Where have you come from and where are you going?" (Genesis 16:8) Sound familiar? She cut quite a forlorn figure, sitting on her own in the desert by a spring. But the king of the universe had noticed, he was there, he could see her, and he would help her.

This is another one of those questions which God already knows the answer to. It's God diving into the process of knowing and being known again. He didn't ask it so he could know about Hagar, he had found her in the desert after all. He asked it because Hagar needed to know she was known by God.

And just like the invalid at the pool of Bethesda, Hagar gives God more than he asks for. She could have just geolocated herself, but she goes for something much more personal than that, "I'm running away from my mistress Sarai." (Genesis 16:8)

As they talk, God hears her story and knows her, he encourages her and tells her what to do next. The story ends with Hagar doing something no one else does in the whole of the Old Testament – she names God. And the name she gave him surprised no one – "You are the God who sees me." (Genesis 16:13) Of course he is.

## BEING SEEN

Sin, shame, and trouble make people invisible. It has always been this way. It was true with Hagar, and it is still true now. They are wrecking balls which crash through human relationships leaving isolated, overlooked, and lonely people in their wake.

Hagar was known by God, and she knew it. He knew where she was, what had happened to her, and he was present with her. He had seen her, and he sees us too. As we commune with him and pour our hearts out to him, he is present with us by his Spirit. In conversation with him through scripture and prayer we engage in knowing and being known by him. He knows us, he knows our context, he is present with us, and we experience being seen by him.

Friends notice one another when they are isolated, overlooked, and alone. They take what they know of their friend's situation and what they know of their friend, and they find a way to be personally present with them. They are the three key elements which need to be present for someone to have the powerful experience of being seen by their friend.

If you want to learn how to see others, then take a close look at how God does it. There is no one better at it than him. He excels at it. He is an outstanding friend.

## SEEING OUTSIDERS

One of the best stories which illustrates the way Jesus notices, knows, and is personally present with isolated people is his interaction with a woman who had a long term, chronic health condition. (Mark 4:24-34) She had been bleeding for twelve years and had sought the assistance of many doctors, but they weren't able to help. Her condition was untreatable. She was out of options, out of money, and out of hope.

To make matters worse, the Old Testament law had something to say about her condition too. It declared her to be unclean as long as she had the issue. She was quite literally an untouchable. It didn't matter whether it was a seat, a bed, or a person, whatever she touched became unclean. She had the same effect on everyone and everything. Her physical problem had created a personal problem. Her condition had isolated her. She was an outsider.

One day, Jesus came along. He was on his way to help a synagogue ruler whose daughter was dying. It was the perfect opportunity for the woman, for someone who was an untouchable, someone who had been pushed to the side, someone who needed to be out of sight and out of mind. She wasn't supposed to touch others, but the size of the crowd provided the perfect cover for her to get close to Jesus. She could be hidden, even lost in a crowd like that. It was the perfect opportunity to sneak a healing.

She would have made many people ceremonially unclean as she pushed her way through the crowd, but she didn't seem to care. She just needed to get to Jesus. She figured that if she could just touch his robe then she would be healed. (Mark 5:28) And she was right.

When she got close enough, she touched his cloak and her bleeding immediately stopped. "It worked!" she must have thought. "Now to melt back into the crowd." But she didn't bargain on what happened next. Jesus turned around and asked, "Who touched my clothes?" And he didn't let it go. He kept looking around and wasn't going to continue on his way until whoever touched him came out of hiding. It was an awkward moment.

Before long, it became obvious she needed to come clean. She couldn't keep it a secret forever. It was a big moment. To publicly talk about such a personal thing with the attached social stigma was bold, even though she didn't have much of a choice. She told Jesus the whole truth in front of the whole crowd.

The pause at the end of her story must have felt like an eternity. A reprimand was due, and Jesus was probably about to give it. At least he should have anyway. But Jesus was up to something completely different. He knew she needed to be seen by him. He knew she had touched him, but her healing, her complete healing needed to go much further than a physical cure. She needed to be seen by Jesus, and he wasn't going to let her go until she had been. "Daughter, your faith has healed you. Go in peace and be freed from your suffering." (Mark 5:34)

If you look closely, you can see the same three ingredients which were present when God met with Hagar in the desert: Jesus had noticed her, she was known by Jesus, and he was personally present with her. She had been seen *and* healed by Jesus. She wouldn't be the same again.

When Jesus called the woman out of the shadows, he was doing what all good friends do. He was actively working against the isolating, sidelining, loneliness-generating effects of shame and trouble. In effect, he was saying to the woman, "Don't stay in there!"

If you are a Christian then he has said this to you multiple times. He said it first when he saved you, and he has said it many times since. Every time sin, shame and trouble cause you to disappear, he sees you and calls you to come out. He is a great friend to you.

We have the opportunity to follow in his footsteps. There are so many people around us who need to be seen by us - our neighbours, our workmates, people at church. There are so many who need a friend who can see them.

## SEEING OTHERS

I want to finish by giving you some practical starting points which will help you to be a friend who sees others. It is important to finish here, because both of the stories we have looked at in this chapter are high-end examples which involve Jesus himself.[5] I don't want that to stop you. There are many simple ways to see those around you. Here are a few to get you started.

### Acknowledge People's Presence

The best starting place for growing in your ability to see people is by getting into the habit of acknowledging their presence. Acknowledging people's presence is as simple as saying something to them when they walk into a room, greeting them when they come and stand near you, or saying hello to them when you look at each other as you walk past them.

We make a habit of acknowledging each other's presence in our family. Angela and I have four sons. The oldest is 20 and the youngest is 15. There is always someone coming or going from our house. But despite the constant comings and goings from sleep-ins, school days, different work shifts, and trips to the gym, we always make a point of acknowledging when someone comes into the main living area of the house. "How was your day?" "How did you go?" "How was work?" Every time we do this we communicate that we see them, and they matter to us.

Acknowledging people's presence is the first step in communicating that you see them. I used to be terrible at this. I just wasn't friendly. I would often walk past people, glance at them, and say nothing. Now I make it my goal to be the first to say hello. Not only is it a thousand times more enjoyable, but it also communicates to others that I see them and they matter to me.

## Pay Attention and Use Your Imagination

If we want to 'see' our friends in whatever they are going through, then we will need to pay attention and use our imagination. When we hear about something which has affected our friend, we will need to take a moment to reflect on and consider what it would be like for them as they walk through it.

Seeing our friends in the midst of what is going on for them will require most of us to slow the pace of our lives down a little to have space for it. Busy people don't always have the headspace to think about what is going on outside of their world because they spend most of their time thinking about what they are doing and the next thing coming their way. I don't mean to imply people are selfish. I just want to highlight the tendency we have to fill our lives up with things at the expense of friendships. It is a tragedy whenever things take precedence over friendships.

Once you have slowed down enough to pay attention to your friends, listen to the words and images they use to describe their inner world. These are powerful clues which will help you to understand how they are experiencing their current situation. If you aren't clear, ask some questions about the situation. Then take what you know of them and what you know of the situation, put them in a bowl in your head (figuratively speaking), and mix them up with your imagination. Spend a few moments thinking about who the real them might be underneath what is happening.

### Be Present with Them

The final step involves finding a way to be present with them in the midst of what is happening. You could call them, or message them, or meet up with them. Each of these methods can communicate to people that you see them. You could say something like this, "I was thinking of you when that happened and thought it might have been …… for you." You fill in the blank. You don't have to write a song or a poem. Just let them know you were thinking of them, and what you were thinking about.

Find a way to be present with them in the place where they feel invisible.

Oh, and one more thing, if someone shares something hard with you, follow up with them in the next day or two. Silence makes people feel invisible too. I have seen this missed opportunity happen too many times. Someone shared something heartbreaking, and the person they shared it with didn't say a word to them until the next organised church event when they saw them again. Asking people how they are going a day or two later, is an easy way to let people know you see them.

## A CONVERSATION BETWEEN FRIENDS

My mate Kurt went to a local supermarket one day to get some food. Upon returning to his car he quickly found out that his power steering had failed. He called for roadside assistance and sat in the car waiting for the tow truck to arrive. As he waited, he called his wife. While he was chatting on the phone to her, the tow truck arrived at the carpark and the driver tried to call him to ask if he could assist in blocking the traffic as he loaded the car. As he talked with his wife, Kurt noticed this call come through but disregarded it because it was a random number that seemed to be from another state in Australia. Unfortunately, it was the tow truck driver's number.

The next thing Kurt saw was the tow truck driver at the end of the carpark yelling at him to get off his (expletive) phone. He was very angry. Kurt got out of his car, stopped the traffic so the truck driver could load his car, and then got in the cab with the truck driver. The first five minutes of the trip was filled with sorrys from Kurt and complaints from the driver about how stupid people are who don't answer calls while they are waiting for tow truck drivers.

Eventually he asked Kurt, "So, what do you do with yourself." Kurt replied, "I'm a minister at a church." Then he went on to share how he had been diagnosed with Parkinson's Disease and needed to change from being a minister to doing pastoral supervision. The driver followed up with some questions about Parkinson's Disease, Kurt's lifestyle, his family, and his kids. It was a clunky start, but Kurt's honest sharing about his weakness completely changed the tenor of the conversation.

The conversation flipped. Kurt asked him about his work and how life had played out for him. He talked about how his dad died of a heart attack when he was 47 years old, his divorce, the aftermath, and how he had become a workaholic. The truck driver was a high output guy, and he was going too hard.

They arrived at their destination, shook hands, and the driver said, "It was good to get to know you."

They weren't friends at the beginning, and most would argue they weren't friends at the end, but when Kurt opened up and was honest about his weakness, the way they were communicating changed. They had opportunity to see and be present with one another in the midst of what they were going through, and it became a lot like a conversation between friends.

She gave this name to the LORD who spoke to her: "You are the God who sees me," for she said, "I have now seen the One who sees me."

Genesis 16:13

## FOR REFLECTION AND DISCUSSION

1) When have you felt seen by someone else?

2) When have you experienced being seen by God?

3) What are a few things you could do to 'see' your non-Christian friends in the middle of what they are walking through?

# 9

# Jesus Cares for Sinners

Don't just stand there, do something.

Ever heard this one? Have you ever said it? Has it ever been said to you?

It usually comes with extra sauce, and the extra sauce is frustration. Those who say it tend to be people who are actively trying to help a situation, and those who it is said to are normally standing by doing nothing. They don't have to save the world. They just need to do something ... anything ... rather than nothing. Because when it comes to helping someone in need, something is better than nothing almost all of the time.

## HUMANITY AND DOING SOMETHING

If you stop and dig a little deeper into this saying, you will notice it tells you a couple of things about humanity.

The first is this: humanity can be prone to doing nothing when doing something should be obvious. Most of you won't need me to spend too much time explaining this one. Almost all of us know what it is like to be on both ends of this saying. Perhaps a few of you are even feeling uncomfortable as you read it because the mere mention of it reminds you of a time when you did nothing, and you should have done something. It was so obvious, it should have been automatic, but it wasn't.

The second is this: when it comes to humanity, doing something to help someone is not always straightforward. This is demonstrated by the fact that while nearly everyone agrees it is good to help someone in need, especially a friend, we don't always follow through. There are times when we don't know what to do, when we fear we will do the wrong thing, when we are too self-interested, when we expect someone else to do it, or when we hesitate because we had a bad experience when we helped someone in the past. These obstacles and others easily get in the way and make helping others more complicated.

## A FIRST CENTURY BLOCKER

One notable blocker to caring for others in the first century was the Jewish religious system. It's ironic, because it was based on the Old Testament law, which could be fulfilled by loving God and loving your neighbour. But instead of the Jew's religious system helping them to love one another, it got in the way of it.

One of the most common flashpoints was around sabbath regulations. One time, when Jesus was teaching in a Synagogue, a woman who had been bent over by a spirit for 18 years was listening to him. (Luke 13:10-17) She just couldn't straighten up! Jesus saw her, called her forward, and healed her. It was incredible. But not everyone was impressed. The leader of the synagogue promptly got up and told everyone to come back on a day which was not the Sabbath if they wanted to be healed. What an anticlimax! His attitude was obvious. He would have done nothing to help on that day if he had the power. His understanding of the religious laws would have stopped him.

Jesus responded to the synagogue leader with the first century version of "Don't just stand there, do something." He took the opportunity to point out how they cared more for their animals on the sabbath than they did for people. (Luke 13:15-16) Ouch.

In the very next chapter there is another sick person, another healing, and another clash with the religious leaders about the sabbath. On this occasion Jesus said, "If one of you has a child or an ox that falls into a well on the Sabbath day, will you not immediately pull it out?" (Luke 14:5) The answer is YES! It's always yes. The Sabbath day is a day for showing mercy, not withholding it. Don't just stand there, do something.

Good friends don't just stand there, they do something. They take the time to know, see, and do something for others. They push through whatever obstacles are in their way in order to do something for their friend. On this count alone, Jesus was an outstanding friend. He was never stalled by blockers, and he never had a single moment in his ministry where he paused to work out whether he would help someone out or not. He just did. He was a magnificent friend.

## JESUS CARED FOR OTHERS

Jesus' life was a catalogue of caring for others. He did it everywhere he went. And it was multi-dimensional too. He healed the sick and demon possessed, he taught people who were like sheep without a shepherd, he touched and healed lepers, he saved the disciples' lives in a storm, he forgave sinners, he fed large numbers of hungry people, he sent an encouraging report to John the Baptist in jail, he helped religious people by rebuking them for their toxic religion, he prayed for children, he cleared out the temple, he defended women from critics, he spent time teaching Nicodemus about who he was, he healed a man's ear which had been cut off in the Garden of Gethsemane, and he cared for Mary and Martha after the death of Lazarus. I could go on. Jesus never stopped caring for others.

One of my favourite examples of Jesus' care is the healing of the man who had been blind since birth. (John 9) At some point in this man's life, Jesus and his disciples passed by. As they did, a discussion ensued about what caused his blindness – was it his sin or his parents'? Someone must have been to blame. But as was so often the case, Jesus was on a different track. The man's blindness wasn't about human responsibility, it was about Jesus and the healing which was about to take place.

Jesus spat on the ground, made mud with the saliva and dirt, and wiped it onto the man's eyes. It was gross, to be sure, but you can't argue about the personal nature of what Jesus did. He then told the man to go and wash

## Jesus Cares for Sinners

in the pool of Siloam. (John 9:6-7) The man went and washed and was instantly healed.

Eventually word gets back to the religious leaders about what Jesus had done. They call the man and his parents in and interrogate them. (John 9:13-34) The pressure applied by the religious leaders caused his parents to distance themselves from their son. The religious leaders then circled back around and had a second rather combative conversation with the formerly blind man which resulted in him being kicked out of the synagogue. (John 9:34) It is a tragic end to what was a stunning miracle.

Culturally all seems lost for the man. He was estranged from his parents and had been removed from the synagogue. He cut an isolated and forsaken figure, someone in need of a friend who would walk alongside him and help him work out what to do next. You know where this is going. Jesus was that friend. He followed him up. A good friend never leaves people alone. Here is how the apostle John introduces the final scene in the story, "Jesus heard that they had thrown him out, and when he found him ..." (John 9:35)

I have often wondered what Jesus was doing when he was interrupted by this news. Probably something important. But true to form, like it always was, it was a welcome interruption for Jesus. He kicked into gear. I imagine him saying to his disciples, "We need to find this man. I need to talk to him." Did he use his unlimited knowledge of everything to find him, or did they split up and do a sweep of the town? We don't know. But the one thing we do know is ... Jesus didn't stand there and do nothing.

Jesus followed up the isolated man. He helped the man to see who he truly was and brought him into his family. Jesus didn't just heal the man's physical eyes. When he followed him up he healed the man's spiritual eyes too. The one who was isolated and alone had been gathered in and was now part of Jesus' family. This sinner, this outsider, became an insider because Jesus was a good friend to him. He was the lost sheep, but the good shepherd had found him.

He wasn't the last lost sheep. There have been countless others since then who have needed to be rescued. We were some of them, and Jesus came and saved us too. He did it in the most stunning of ways, by being crucified on a Roman cross. It was the breathtaking fulfillment of the promise God made at the fall, "Someone will come for you." And he did. But the good news is that as good as the cross was, it wasn't the end of his saving work. His coming once, his dying on the cross for us, guaranteed he would come a thousand times. (Rom 8:32) He won't lose you. He will care for you. When you need him to rescue you, he will be there; I have no doubt.

## BEING A FRIEND TO OTHERS

When it comes to being a friend to those who don't know Jesus, and anyone for that matter, here are three simple ways you can care for others: check in with them, follow them up, and when all else fails, just do something.

## Check In

All of us have times where we have others on our mind, but we don't always let them know or ask them how they are going. Checking in is about taking the initiative to find out how your friend is. A check in involves you taking the initiative to connect with them and find out how they are going.

One of my friends checked in on me the other day. I missed his call, but he left a message, "Hi mate. Just calling to check in on how you are going. Give me a call when you have a chance." He wasn't calling about anything in particular, he just wanted to know how I was going. It was a simple action which made me feel cared for.

Check-ins can be more specific too. If you have heard somehow about something which is happening for your friend, get on the front foot and check in with them about how they are going with it. Ask them what effect it is having on them or what they think about what is happening. "When I heard what happened at work, I wondered how you went with that?" Or if you know them quite well, you could suggest the way you think they would be handling it. "I imagine what just happened at home would make you feel nervous about going back to work next week."

## Follow-Up

Following up is something you do in response to a conversation you had previously with your friend. It may be that they shared something significant, hard, or confusing with you, and sometime later you let them know you have been wondering how they are going or how they are travelling in the midst of what they shared with you. Checking in is proactive, following up is reactive.

The power in follow-up lies in carrying other people on our hearts. (2 Timothy 1:3-4) To be remembered is to be cared for. Have you ever felt cared for when someone followed-up with you? I have. Especially when they asked me about something I had assumed they would have forgotten about. When they follow up with me I often find myself thinking, "Oh, you remembered. You must have had me on your mind." To be thought of, to be on someone's heart when they are not with you, is sublime indeed.

Following up with your friends is one of the most simple ways you can care for them. It doesn't normally take very long – just a quick message or a short phone call to ask how they are going. Here's a good rule of thumb: the more urgent or difficult the matter, the quicker you need to follow them up after the initial conversation. The less urgent the matter, the more time you have. So, follow up with others, and take the opportunity to care for them. Don't let the personal thing your friend shared with you slip your mind.

## Do Something

Finally, if all else fails, then just do something. Doing something is almost always better than doing nothing.

If you have a heart to get beside your friend and walk with them, and you have some idea of what you can do, then go ahead and try it. Cook a meal, send a message, make the phone call, take them out for coffee, drop in and see them. Imagine what would be helpful to you if you were in their situation and then go and do it for them.

Friends lean in. They aren't overbearing or pushy, but they don't wait to be asked either. There aren't many things which are unhelpful, so go ahead and try something. As you do, just be sensitive to their feedback about what is helpful and what isn't. If you communicate your heart for them as you do it, then the old adage normally wins the day – it's the thought that counts.

Finally, here's another good rule of thumb: the more personal the help you give, the more likely it will be helpful to others. Help which hits the mark more powerfully tends to be help which reveals the heart of the person seeking to care for their friend. Here are a couple of examples:

1) When you shoot off an encouragement or a question to check how your friend is going, let them know they have been on your mind. Making connections between their life and yours communicates to them that they matter to you. Building friendships can be as simple as making these kinds of personal connections.

2) Offering to pray for people. Now this one may seem a little strange, but I have offered to pray for non-Christians on many occasions and have never been rejected – not even once. In my experience, all of them have appreciated my care in doing so.

Sometimes I will pray with them in person if I am confident it will go down okay, other times I will offer to pray for them when we are apart. Depending on the friendship, you might even get the opportunity to let them know what you are praying for them and how it is connected to your heart for them.

## A CONVERSATION BETWEEN FRIENDS

I remember a time when we went camping at the beach and a man called Rob and his family were camping next door to us. Before retiring he was a first responder who had been in charge of the station he was posted at. Rob was an extrovert. He enjoyed talking with new people and was keen to learn whatever he could from whoever he met.

Rob popped over to introduce himself shortly after we finished our setup. Our initial interaction had all of the typical features of those who are meeting each other for the first time. We shook hands, told each other our names, asked about where each other lived, what family we had, and what paid work we were engaged in. He seemed genuinely interested in what my wife and I did and wasn't put off by our involvement in church even though by his own admission, he wasn't a 'church person.'

A couple of days later he dropped in for another chat. He wanted to know where our church was and how my wife and I had started it. Before long we were talking about what it was like to work with volunteers. Both of us had experience in leading them – he in his oversight of volunteer first responders and me in the local church.

We went on and talked about what it was like to lead volunteers and how you needed to be careful in the way you exercised authority and power over them. He said, "Heavy handedness and steamrolling people with power and authority doesn't get you where you really want to go." To which I added, "We can't get away with doing that anyway. Because it is not the way Jesus used power and authority. Jesus didn't come down on top of people, he got down low and lifted people up. That's the best way to help people." He wholeheartedly agreed. I added, "There is nothing more powerfully transformative than when someone sacrifices themselves for the good of someone else. That's exactly what Jesus did for humanity."

He was straight onto it. He knew exactly what I meant and immediately told me a story from his days as the head of his station. He and his men had been called to attend the location where a suicide had taken place. By his own admission, it was an ugly scene which he found particularly disturbing. The next day at work he followed up with the men who had joined him the day before. He asked, "How did you go last night? Were you able to eat dinner?" They replied, "Yep. We were okay. No worries." He said, "I wasn't. I could only have toast for dinner." He was putting himself out there for the good of his team. They quickly responded by saying they weren't any good either. Toast was the only food they could manage to eat too.

Did you notice what Rob did? He went out on a limb, he was personal and vulnerable with his team, in order to care for them. And his being personal with them opened up the space for them to talk about how they truly were. It was beautiful work. I said to Rob, "That was a good thing you did for them. You put yourself on the line to care for them. That's just what we were talking about." Rob did something to care for his team. He didn't need to, but he got down low and lifted them up.

I hadn't met Rob before and may not ever see him again. But as we talked about how we had cared for the people under us, Jesus' sacrificial death naturally came up. It wasn't weird or forced and he didn't recoil, it was just a conversation between friends.

> Greater love has no one than this: to lay down one's life for one's friends.
>
> John 15:13

### FOR REFLECTION AND DISCUSSION

1) When have you done nothing when you should have done something?

2) Who cares for you? What kinds of things do they do to communicate it to you?

3) What are all the ways Jesus cares for you? How can you care for others?

## 10

## Jesus is Loyal to Sinners

Last night, at the end of dinner, I asked my teenage boys if they could help me with this book. I told them I needed some ideas from them about friendship. They were keen so I asked them, "How do you be a good friend to others?" They immediately said, "If one of your friends gets in a fight, you don't leave them alone. You go and help them." You need to know my boys love, watch, and play contact sports.

I was hoping for something a little less violent. So I asked them again, "Okay. I get that. What else would you say?" They then said, "If someone is against your friend, then they are against you. You never leave your friend on their own. You always get behind them and support them if something is going down."

Now, in spite of the combative nature of how they expressed it, I wonder if you can hear what they are saying? It's actually quite clear. For them, friendship is all about loyalty. I asked a few follow up questions in an effort to get something else out of them, but they kept coming back to the same thing. From their perspective, there was no other answer. Being a friend is about loyalty, solidarity, constant support, and allegiance. It's about being together and protecting one another from people who are against you, and it isn't about anything else ... well, at least not last night anyway. I think they had a point.

They didn't use the word love. They wouldn't, because they are teenage boys. But everything they were saying had to do with love. Loyalty is all about love, active love. It is about being and staying together. It is about staying tight relationally. Loyalty is about loving your friend, being for them in every situation, and always acting in your friend's best interest. You won't find the word loyalty or loyal in the bible very much, but you can't love someone without it.

There may be no better definition of loyalty between friends than the wise saying of Proverbs 17:17: "A friend loves at all times." That's a loyalty definition in six words. It sums it up. If you put these glasses on when you read scripture, you will see loyalty everywhere – faithfulness, covenant, bearing one another's burdens and so on. Love is flat and lifeless without it.

## THE ENEMY OF LOYALTY

Take a look at the life of Jesus through the lenses of loyalty and you will quickly discover the arch enemy of loyalty - religion. The basic premise of this book is an indicator of it. The nickname, friend of sinners, was given to Jesus by religious people. Their intention was to expose Jesus as being loyal to sinners in a way which was wrong. In their mind, their loyalties were well placed; his though, were a disaster.

Religious people, by and large, are not loyal to people, they are loyal to systems – religious systems. Or, in the case of the first century Jewish leaders, the law of Moses and their interpretations of it. Religious systems and the people within them support others in the system when they comply with it, and they distance themselves from them when they aren't or don't. The loyalty in religion is to the system, not to people, because at the heart, it isn't about loyalty. It is about compliance. When people comply, they fit in, when they don't, they are out.

When Jesus came, he fulfilled the law *and* he was loyal to people. He showed how the heart of God's law is personal in nature from start to finish. That's why the commands can be boiled down to the love of God and the love of neighbour. In Jesus' life we see how the fulfillment of the law and loyalty to people are not at odds with one another – they simply aren't an either/or proposition. It is about loving God *and* your neighbour. God's heart within the law, when viewed correctly, should make us a better friend not a worse one. Whenever religion runs amuck in a church, systems will take precedence over people, and loyalty will be in short supply.

It may be just me, but loyalty between church members has not been a strong emphasis in any church I have been a part of. In most cases, it has been entirely absent. If you can identify with this, then I have good news for you. There has never been a more loyal friend to sinners than Jesus. If we want to learn how to be loyal friends, then we will need to return to our roots – Jesus himself.

## THE LOYAL FRIEND

Jesus is a loyal friend from start to finish. From his incarnation to his death, his support of and allegiance to sinners is clear and well-documented. He is *the* friend who loves at all times.

Take the story of Zaccheus for example. He was a chief tax collector. If there was ever someone who embodied disloyalty, it was Zaccheus. Tax collectors were Jewish people who worked for the Romans, collecting taxes from their own people. They would routinely rip them off for their own personal gain. Zaccheus was a chief tax collector and he wanted to see Jesus. Upon hearing that Jesus was passing by, he climbed a tree to see him. But instead of walking past, Jesus walked straight up to him and invited himself over to his house. The mutterings of those watching on were a dead giveaway that loyalty was in play, "He has gone to be the guest of a sinner." (Luke 19:7) If friendship is about loyalty, and loyalty is about who you associate with in the face of opposition, then Jesus was a good friend to Zaccheus. Jesus' loyalty to him changed his life.

Another example of Jesus' loyalty was to the woman who had been crippled, the one who had been bent over by the demon for 18 years. (Luke 13:10-17) Remember her? She was the one who had been healed. She was also

## Jesus is Loyal to Sinners

the one who the synagogue leader was publicly shaming when he told the crowd to come back on a day other than the Sabbath if they wanted to be healed. Don't miss what is going on here. Take careful note of what the religious leader was up to: he was using his power to criticise the woman and pull the rest of the crowd back into line with his religious system.

Anyone who knew Jesus would have been able to predict what he was going to do next. Can you? Let me give you a hint. Here's what we know about Jesus: he never leaves anyone isolated and alone. So, it comes as no surprise to us to find him getting involved. He rebuked the leader for his inconsistency and defended the woman. "Should not this woman, a daughter of Abraham, whom Satan has kept bound for eighteen long years, be set free on the Sabbath day from what bound her?" (Luke 13:16) It's a sweet moment. She would have had a smile on her face from ear to ear. Not just because she was healed, but because of the way Jesus defended her. (Luke 13:17)

Other times, Jesus expressed his loyalty by having hard conversations with people. One of the most powerful pictures of this is the restoration and reinstatement of Peter. Despite Peter's assurances of his loyalty to Jesus, he did just as Jesus predicted he would – on the night before his crucifixion, Peter denied he knew Jesus three times. After the third and final denial, Luke adds a gut-wrenching note, "The Lord turned and looked straight at Peter." (Luke 22:61) This was a big moment. Surely there could be no coming back from this.

But Jesus is a loyal friend. He is for the disciples, even

and perhaps especially, when they were wrong. One of his appearances after his resurrection was on the shore of the sea of Galilee. A group of the disciples had been fishing all night, and he was waiting with a cooked breakfast for them. (John 21:9) They were deserters and deniers, yet he turned up for them. He fed them, associated himself with them, and loved them. Jesus' loyalty to them was on display.

But this time around, his loyalty went even further. Because it wasn't enough for the disciple Peter to know he was forgiven for denying Jesus, he needed to be reinstated, he needed to be restored. Like a skilled surgeon, Jesus went straight to work removing the gangrenous area of failure by asking him the same question three times, until it hurt – "Do you love me?" (John 21:15-17) It was a mirror image of what had happened not long before, an opportunity for Peter to set the record straight. And it was just what he needed. Jesus' loyalty to Peter didn't stop with his forgiveness of him, it led to and found expression in a hard, but restorative conversation.

All these expressions of Jesus' loyalty were just shadows of the greatest act of loyalty ever - his death on the cross for sinners. It was sublime and outrageous, brutal and beautiful, exactly what sinners needed, yet not what they deserved. It was love and loyalty on display in a way which had never been seen before nor would ever be seen again.

It shouldn't have been a surprise; it was what Jesus was saying and doing all the way along. The night before his death on the cross, he taught his disciples, "Greater love has no one than this: to lay down one's life for one's

## Jesus is Loyal to Sinners

friends." (John 15:13) Jesus said what everyone knew: the quality of your loyalty and love is directly connected to what you give up for your friend. The greater the personal sacrifice, the more powerful the loyalty, the deeper the love. And there is nothing of greater value to anyone than their life.

While Jesus' love for his friends is similar to many others' who have died for their friends, there is something which takes his sacrifice into the stratosphere – he didn't just die for his friends, he died for his enemies. This is a whole different level of loyalty. The apostle Paul highlights this distinction in Romans 5:7-8. He says what most of us are thinking; someone perhaps might die for a righteous or good person, but no one lays their life down for evil people. It just doesn't happen. Unless you are God. "God shows his love for us in that while we were still sinners, Christ died for us." (Romans 5:8)

Jesus loved us when we didn't love him. (Romans 5:10) He was a friend to us when we were an enemy to him. His death on the cross will stand for all time as the ultimate expression of love for a friend. As he hung there on the cross, being mocked, struggling for air, pain coursing through his body, carrying our sins on the tree, he said to the world and he said to you, "Friend, I love you." Then he died. Jesus ... a loyal friend of sinners.

## A LOYAL FRIEND

As we consider what loyalty looks like with respect to those who don't know Jesus yet, we need to make sure we don't fall into the trap of thinking that loyalty to God and loyalty to sinners are at odds with one another. They weren't with Jesus. He was completely loyal to his Father and truly loyal to sinners. He embodied the love of God and the love of neighbour by showing they aren't at odds with one another but fit naturally alongside each other. We shouldn't be surprised. The prophet Isaiah described him as the high and exalted one who dwells with the contrite and lowly. (Isaiah 57:15)

I want to briefly look at four ways Jesus showed loyalty to sinners and how we can too: associating with them, defending them, speaking truth to them, and living out the gospel in front of them.

### Associating

This one is quite straightforward. If we are to show loyalty to those who don't know Jesus yet, then we will need to associate with them. A siege mentality will not do. Some of us don't have them, but all of us need to have friends who don't know Jesus yet. And I don't mean people who are a ministry or an evangelism project. I mean genuine friends. They don't have to be your best friends, but they need to be a friend. And don't just grin and bear it. Get amongst it and enjoy them. There are lots of wonderful people out there.

### Defending

When you hear about some trouble coming at your friend, get in alongside them, better yet, get out in front of them and do what you can to defend them from what is happening to them. If there is an opportunity to actively engage with what is coming their way then do it. If there isn't, then defend them to their face. Tell them how terrible it is and how upset you are about what is happening to them. If you end up in a conversation with someone who knows about it, make it clear to them who you are aligned with.

Your friend may not handle it the way you think they should, but you can back them anyway and talk about it with them afterwards. No one ever gets everything right. There is a time to nuance things, but it is not normally when your friend is under attack. That is the time to communicate solidarity, the time to be tight, the time to be together. Be for your friends wherever you go, because "a friend loves at all times."

## Speaking Truth

Being loyal will sometimes involve saying things to your friend which they don't necessarily want to hear. A good friend always says something when their friend is headed down the wrong path. But just be careful about your timing. Cutting across people before they are convinced of your loyalty to them is risky. Remember, the words of a friend are always heartfelt and sweet, even and perhaps especially, when they disagree. (Proverbs 27:9) If they know you have their back, then there will be a time and place when you will be able to offer something to them which is different to what they think. And when you do, remember you are a friend engaging in a dialogue, not a preacher delivering a monologue.

If loyalty is about loving your friends and wanting the best for them, then you will pray for them and talk about Jesus with them from time to time. If you never talk about Jesus with your non-Christian friends, then you have a loyalty problem in your relationship with Jesus because you won't stick with him publicly, and you have a loyalty problem with your friends because you won't tell them about the saviour of the world, the best friend they could ever have. You don't have to force it or get weird about it. You just need to be honest about who he is and what he means to you.

## Living Out the Gospel

Jesus laid his life down so we could have life. It was a pattern which was well established from the incarnation and found ultimate fulfillment on the cross. And he invited all those who wanted to follow him to live a life which was gospel shaped. And while it is a unique call to all those who seek to follow him, it is also the DNA of all true friendships. It is the template of the kind of friend we need to be to those who don't know him yet.

When your friend is in need, give up whatever you are doing or want to be doing, let go of the life you could have, so you can give it to your friend. Give up your time to call or drop in and see your friend, give up your money by being generous and paying for their dinner, and if it came down to it, give up your life for them. The shape and rhythm of the gospel is what makes all true friendships go, whether people know it or not. Know I am praying with you that your non-Christian friends enjoy your giving life to them and come to see the gospel through it one day.

## A CONVERSATION BETWEEN FRIENDS

I remember writing a 10 000-word journal article a few years ago. I worked hard on it, thought it was headed in the right direction and sent it off to my good friend to give me some feedback.

Not long after I sent it, he called me. His opening question was, "Do you want me to say what I really think about what you have written?" I paused internally for a moment. I needed to gather myself because if I said yes, I knew it was going to hurt. His question gave him away. On a superficial level, I didn't really want to hear what he had to say, but I remembered his loving loyalty to me and how he consistently has my best interests at heart, so I said "Yes. I do want to hear what you think." Then he said, "Well. You need to throw out two thirds of it. It is no good. And you need to turn the left over bit into the whole paper."

He was right. Two thirds of it wasn't any good. I set about doing a rewrite, and it was that rewrite which has become the foundation for much of what I have written since.

My mate was lovingly loyal to me. He didn't tell me what I wanted to hear; he told me what I needed to hear. It was a hard conversation, but it was a conversation between friends.

> A friend loves at all times.
>
> Proverbs 17:17

## FOR REFLECTION AND DISCUSSION

1) What are some practical ways you can be loyal to those around you who don't know Jesus yet?

2) How has Jesus been loyal to you?

3) What has been your experience of loyalty within the church?

# 11

# A Final Word

You have a friend.

*You have always had a friend.*

Jesus is the friend all of us need. He came to us at our worst and walked with us. He didn't come only to pay our sin-debt and get us out of a bind – as crucial as that is. He came to be our friend and to invite us into a friendship with him. A powerfully transformative friendship which makes you a better friend than you have ever been.

I began the book by looking at the nickname the religious leaders gave to Jesus - friend of sinners - before going on to unpack how he lived it out. The religious leaders thought they were on to a winner with their taunt. They thought the nickname nailed him down and summed him up. And they were right. It summed him up perfectly, just not the way they intended it. The slander which they hoped would harass him became the life-giving hope of all those who would ever come to him. For those people it was the best news ever.

All true friendships bear the marks of his friendship with us. They all have an outside-in direction to them. People who are good friends connect with others and bring them into the relational circles in which they move, and Jesus is no different. Except that his friendship extends further out than any friendship has ever done and it brings people further in than anyone else ever could. His friendship moves us from isolated fallen sinners into the very community of the trinity. You can't be any more in than that.

My main objective in writing this book was for you to see Jesus and be drawn to him. I did this because I really like him, and I want you to like him too. I wanted you to see how he rolled and be drawn to him – perhaps even for the first time. I didn't want the book to be mainly about you or me and what we are doing; I wanted it to be about him. I wanted you to make the connections between his friendship of others and his friendship of you so you could make the connection between his friendship of you and your friendships with those around you.

You have read this book because the only real insider took on human flesh and was a friend to you, and brought you in. It is simultaneously stunning and outrageous, tailor-made yet something no one expected. Little did humanity know who would be the fulfilment of the ancient proverb, "There is a friend who sticks closer than a brother." (Proverbs 18:24)

**A Final Word**

*Jesus, a friend of sinners.*

*Jesus, a friend of* _____.
   *(insert your name here)*

# Endnotes

1. https://www.who.int/teams/social-determinants-of-health/demographic-change-and-healthy-ageing/social-isolation-and-loneliness

2. Names and identifying details have been changed to protect people's privacy

3. https://www.news.com.au/travel/travel-updates/incidents/two-chinese-climbers-abandon-dream-summit-to-rescue-dying-woman/news-story/05c68a-631c5a8c117939f42d4e1e3aa2.

4. In scripture, the ultimate expression of people knowing and being known by God is their being restored to right relationship with him through Jesus. When I talk about Jesus knowing sinners in this chapter, I am not referring to their salvation, but to Jesus engaging in the relational mechanism of knowing and being known.

5. As you can see in the story of Hagar, interactions with the Angel of the Lord in the Old Testament appear to be interactions with God himself.

www.ingramcontent.com/pod-product-compliance
Lightning Source LLC
Chambersburg PA
CBHW062050290426
44109CB00027B/2782